ON TRIAL

The Case of Keli Lane
and the ABC

SIMON DAVIS

BIRRIEBUNGIE PRESS

ON TRIAL: The Case of Keli Lane and the ABC
Simon Davis
www.simondavis.com.au
www.facebook.com/SimonDavisAuthor
simon140860@bigpond.com

First published in Australia by Birriebungie Press 2019

A catalogue record for this
book is available from the
National Library of Australia

NATIONAL
LIBRARY
OF AUSTRALIA

ISBN: 978-0-6481252-2-8 (pbk)
ISBN: 978-0-6481252-3-5 (ebk)

Subjects: TRUE CRIME/Murder/General
AW/Media and the Law
LANGUAGE ARTS AND DISCIPLINES/Journalism

Typesetting and design by Publicious Book Publishing
Published in collaboration with Publicious Book Publishing
www.publicious.com.au

The proceeds of this book will be shared with a women's and children's refuge on the South Coast of New South Wales, as is the case with the proceeds of my first book. If and when baby safe havens are introduced into Australia, as in other parts of the world, these proceeds will be diverted to that cause.

DEDICATION

This book is dedicated to my beloved wife, Kathryn, who has once again supported me unconditionally through the demanding journey of writing a book.

TABLE OF CONTENTS

Cast of Characters and Glossary of Terms and Acronyms

(pseudonyms used for some persons)

ABC	Australian Broadcasting Corporation
ABERNETHY, John	State Coroner
ACPE	Australian College of Physical Education
ADAMSON, Justice Christine	Justice of New South Wales Court of Criminal Appeal
AM1	A gentleman by the name of Andrew Morris who gave evidence on the *voir dire* at Keli Lane's trial, and was interviewed by the ABC documentary *Exposed: The Case of Keli Lane*
ANDREATTA, Lisa	Witness, friend of Keli Lane
ANGLICARE	Anglicare Adoption Services
ARCHBOLD, Ben	Solicitor who represented Keli Lane at trial in 2010
BAKER, Huw	Counsel for prosecution, junior to Tedeschi QC
BALDWIN, Clayton	Acquaintance of Duncan Gillies
BALTRA-VASQUEZ, Alicia	Social worker
BATHURST, Chief Justice Tom	Chief Justice of Supreme Court of New South Wales

BELL, Justice Virginia	Justice of High Court of Australia
BUIST, Professor Anne	Psychiatrist
BOROVNIK, John	Employee of Department of Community Services
CAINS, Peter	Keli Lane's first husband (married in 2000)
CCA	New South Wales Court of Criminal Appeal
CENTACARE	Centacare Adoption Agency
CHAPPLE SC, Keith	Defence senior counsel (trial)
CHEN, Dr Stephen	Doctor at Auburn Hospital
CHIN, Rachael Jane	Author, observer at trial
CLARK, Peter	Occupant of Unit 11, 24 Wisbeach Street, Balmain
CLARK, Steven	Occupant of Unit 11, 24 Wisbeach Street, Balmain
COWDERY QC, Nicholas	Director of Public Prosecutions
DIAMOND, Dr Michael	Psychiatrist
DOCS	New South Wales Department of Community Services
DURAISAMY, Ms	Witness
FREEDMAN, Mia	Media personality
FUNG, Virginia	Employee of Anglicare
GAUT, Detective Richard	Police officer
GILLIES, Duncan	Boyfriend of Keli Lane
GIRDHAM, Jennie SC	Senior Counsel for the Crown in Keli Lane's appeals to the New South Wales Court of Criminal Appeal and High Court of Australia
GREAVES, Sean	Occupant of Unit 10, 24 Wisbeach Street, Balmain
HABIB, Debra Lee	Social worker
HAMILL SC, Peter	Counsel represented Keli Lane at inquest in 2005

HANLON, Ann	Registered nurse at Auburn Hospital
HCA	High Court of Australia
HENSON, Darryl	Witness
HOLT, Kati	Friend of Keli Lane
HOWARD, Alan	Pseudonym of father of Archie, born on 31 May 1999
KGV Hospital	King George V Hospital
KEANE, Justice Patrick	Justice of High Court of Australia
KEHOE, Detective Mathew	Police officer
KILANI, Detective Tamer	Police officer
LANE, Archie	Pseudonym of Keli Lane's child born on 31 May 1999
LANE, Keli	Convicted for murder of two day old Tegan Lee Lane
LANE, Morgan	Brother of Keli Lane
LANE, Rob	Father of Keli Lane
LANE, Sandra	Mother of Keli Lane
LANE, Tegan Lee	Murder victim
LANE, Trisha	Pseudonym of Keli Lane's first child, born in 1995
LANGDON, Allison	Journalist, author
LAWRENCE, Kara	Journalist
LATHAM, Justice Megan	Justice of Supreme Court of New South Wales
LAURIE, Kathryn	Solicitor who represented Keli at trial in 2010
McCARTNEY, Narelle	Pseudonym of witness and friend of Keli Lane
MONTGOMERY, Dr Debra	Psychiatrist
MILOVANOVICH, Carl	Coroner, inquest in 2004
MORRIS, Andrew	Witness
NICHOLSON, Elizabeth	Junior Counsel for Keli Lane in appeal to High Court of Australia

QC	Queen's Counsel
RDMP	Ryde Domiciliary Midwife Program
RHODES, Sharon	Ex police officer
ROBERTS, Paul	Pseudonym of Manly rugby footballer who fathered Keli Lane's first child born in 1995
RUYTERS, Dr Michele	Director of Royal Melbourne Institute of Technology Bridge of Hope Innocence Initiative
SC	Senior Counsel
SIMPSON, Justice Carolyn	Justice of New South Wales Court of Criminal Appeal
SLOANE, Sylvie	Counsel, junior to Chapple SC at trial in 2010
TEDESCHI QC, Mark	Senior Crown Prosecutor
TERRACINI SC, Winston	Senior Counsel acted for Keli Lane in appeals
THOMPSON, Dr Jeremy	Keli Lane's general practitioner
TOWNSEND, Sheila	Social worker
TREVALLION, James	Junior counsel to Terracini SC in appeals
TYACK, Aaron	Boyfriend of Keli Lane
WHEALY, Justice Anthony	Trial judge
WISBEACH	24 Wisbeach Street, Balmain

INTRODUCTION

On 13 December 2010, in a media fanfare, Keli Lane (hereafter "Keli") was convicted for the murder of her two day old child, Tegan Lane. The Crown had alleged the murder occurred on 14 September 1996. Tegan has never been seen since that day. Keli was the last person verified as having seen Tegan or having been with her. This is the story of Keli and her trial and conviction. It is also a story about how the media can appear to impugn the decisions of the courts and diminish confidence in the rule of law. This book is, in part, a fact-check of various claims made in a documentary broadcasted by the Australian Broadcasting Corporation ("ABC") in 2018. The documentary was entitled *Exposed: The Case of Keli Lane ("Exposed")*.

Having watched Exposed, and knowing little else about the case, I was left with impressions that, amongst other things, the Crown prosecutor at Keli's trial was guilty of misconduct, that improper deals were done to keep witnesses from testifying and that Keli's lawyers were negligent. I practiced law for a long time and I am aware the courts deliver flawed outcomes from time to time. But I never saw anything quite like this. It was hard to fathom how Keli could have been convicted. A quick look at social media revealed an uproar about the failure of the administration of criminal justice in New South Wales as a result of what was broadcasted by *Exposed*. Curiosity triggered, I turned to read the available factual material, including transcripts, judgments and Coronial findings. I also drew on my own experience as a solicitor and barrister, as I have done in writing this book. Much can be gleaned about events from the way in which the associated litigation is conducted. For example, in this case, the absence of certain submissions in the trial and subsequent appeals was telling. The views and conclusions that I have formed and expressed in this book represent my opinions following my review of the factual material.

Many of the persons involved in the events had their names suppressed by court order. The effect of those orders is continuing. Accordingly, pseudonyms have been used in respect of those persons.

I would like to acknowledge the assistance of Jean Harwood in the production of this book.

I also wish to thank Andy McDermott and his team at Publicious Book Publishing Services for the cover design, printing, typesetting and general production of the book.

Finally, I would like to thank the friends I met through social media for their camaraderie, support and assistance.

CHAPTER 1 - The Story

Background

Keli was born on 21 March 1975. Her childhood was unremarkable. She lived with her family at Fairlight which is a suburb near Manly in Sydney's northern beaches area. She attended Mackellar Girls High School at Manly Vale.

Keli excelled at sport, and would become an elite water polo player in her teens and early 20's. Her parents, Rob and Sandra Lane, were reasonably well known in the Manly area. Rob was a local police officer and coached the Manly rugby team in the 1980's. Keli has a brother named Morgan. The Lane family unit appears to me not unlike many suburban Australian families.

Keli's First Pregnancy

In 1992, Keli was 17 years old and she became pregnant to her boyfriend, Aaron Tyack. Keli and Aaron agreed to terminate the pregnancy and this happened in November 1992. The experience was traumatic. Aaron told an *Exposed* interviewer that Keli was "*shattered*"[1].

Second Pregnancy

In November 1993, Keli fell pregnant again. She was 18 years old. She was still in a relationship with Aaron, but it was not clear he was the father on this occasion. My research has left me unclear as to the

---

[1] *Exposed,* Episode 1, at 0.21. All references are drawn from the documentary as it was originally broadcasted in Australia on ABC television in September and October 2018.

identity of the father. In March 1994, Keli underwent a termination. She was 20 weeks pregnant. She again found it traumatic. It was something that she wanted to avoid doing again[2].

Third Pregnancy

Between April and June 1994, Keli commenced a relationship with a Manly rugby footballer, Duncan Gillies (hereafter "Duncan"). Also, in June, Keli became pregnant again, not to Duncan but to another footballer by the name of Paul Roberts (Roberts' paternity was later discovered by DNA testing). It is difficult to work out but Roberts appears to have been Keli's boyfriend in between, or overlapping with, the relationships with Aaron Tyack and Duncan. At any rate, all boyfriends remained unaware of this pregnancy[3].

On 19 March 1995, at King George V Hospital ("KGV Hospital"), Keli delivered a healthy female baby who she named Trisha. She had earlier commenced labour while socialising at a pub in Balmain and attended Balmain Hospital. Keli told Balmain Hospital staff she was from Perth and had been in Sydney for three weeks. Keli gave the name of a Perth obstetrician under whose care she claimed to have been. None of this was true. At KGV Hospital, she told staff she had ante-natal care in Perth, her parents were in Perth, she had no support in Sydney and she had been living at Harbord, all of which was false. Keli told other lies to the KGV Hospital staff, too many to set out here. Duncan was unaware of Keli having given birth.

This was the beginning of a pattern of lying and deception by Keli on a grand scale, as will be seen. It has been estimated Keli told no less than 95 lies or half-truths to various persons and agencies about her pregnancies.

On 23 March 1995, Keli was discharged from KGV Hospital but left Trisha at the hospital, having surrendered her for adoption. Keli told a social worker, Debra Habib, that she was a representative water polo

---

[2] *Exposed*, Episode 1, at 0.24ff.

[3] It will be seen that Keli was able to keep her pregnancies secret from all around her. Whilst some claim to have suspected Keli was pregnant, most had no inkling whatsoever.

player and her ambition was to compete in the 2000 Sydney Olympic Games. She said she did not feel in a position to parent a child.

Keli was referred to the Centacare Adoption Agency ("Centacare") where she came into contact with another social worker, Sheila Townsend. Keli told Ms Townsend that she wanted to pursue water polo and *"missed out on national selection last year because of another pregnancy"*.

The adoption of Trisha was not smooth sailing. Keli conveyed a number of falsehoods to Ms Townsend including the following:

- she had moved to Perth at age 13;
- her parents lived in Perth;
- she attended school and university in Perth;
- her parents were aware of the pregnancy and, although not happy, were supportive;
- Duncan was the father of Trisha;
- Duncan was willing to sign adoption papers but he was in the United Kingdom and not due back for two weeks;
- she and Duncan had moved from Perth to Sydney three weeks before the birth; and
- Duncan had visited Keli and Trisha in hospital and hugged and kissed Trisha.

Ms Townsend emphasised to Keli the need for Duncan to be involved in the adoption process. Keli told Ms Townsend she was under pressure from Duncan because she had previously promised she would not involve him. Keli eventually indicated that Duncan had agreed to visit Centacare with her. But when Keli next attended, Duncan was not with her. She explained that Duncan had gone to Scotland to play rugby. This was false. Duncan remained unaware of the birth.

On 3 April 1995, Keli swore (signed on oath) an affidavit for the purposes of Supreme Court adoption proceedings[4]. The affidavit

---

[4] Unless otherwise stated, "Supreme Court" means the Supreme Court of New South Wales.

contained a number of untruths including the following statement about Duncan:

> *"He has indicated to me his willingness to sign . . . a consent [for adoption of Trisha]. At the present time he is working in the United Kingdom and has plans to return within the next 14 days"*

This statement, and the other untruths in the affidavit, would later give rise to the first of three charges of perjury (later replaced by charges of false swearing [lying on oath] – I shall refer to these as "false swearing" charges).

During April and May 1995, Keli's quest to keep the birth and adoption secret from Duncan became quite crazed. Keli had given a false address and phone number to Ms Townsend. On about 17 April, Ms Townsend wrote to the address given by Keli (3/20 Ocean View Road, Harbord) and asked her to contact the agency because the phone number appeared to be incorrect. The Harbord address did not in fact exist. Therefore, presumably, Keli did not receive Ms Townsend's letter. Nothing was heard from Keli. On 27 April, Ms Townsend sent a letter by registered post to Duncan at 3/20 Ocean View Road, Harbord. The letter enclosed the adoption application and papers for Duncan to sign. Letters sent by registered post need to be collected and signed for at the receiving Post Office.

On 29 April 1995, Keli attended Centacare and told Ms Townsend that everything was out of control and she and Duncan had separated. Keli said Duncan was claiming she had tricked him by telling he did not have to be involved. Apart from being out of control, everything said by Keli was false. On that day, Keli swore another affidavit that included these lies, together with false statements that Duncan had changed his mind and no longer wanted any involvement with Trisha. The false statements in this affidavit would later afford the basis of the second charge of false swearing. It seems to have been on this day that Keli also learned that Ms Townsend had sent the letter by registered post to Duncan. On 5 May, Keli went to Harbord Post Office and collected the letter. Duncan never saw it.

On 10 May 1995, Keli falsely told Centacare that Duncan had received the letter and they would be discussing it that night. On 12 May, Ms Townsend queried the phone number Keli had given for herself. Keli insisted it was correct. On 15 May, Ms Townsend tried the number again but was again told it was a wrong number. On 17 May, Ms Townsend again wrote to Duncan at 3/20 Ocean View Road, Harbord and stated in the letter that she had been informed that he had received the registered post about the adoption. Ms Townsend invited Duncan to contact the agency. Also on 17 May, Keli told Ms Townsend that Duncan was aware of the agency trying to contact him and he wanted it to stop harassing him. Keli also insisted she had given Ms Townsend the correct phone number. She claimed that the person answering the number she had given was one of Duncan's flatmates who was lying for him. All of this was false. On 31 May, Keli told Ms Townsend she had little contact with Duncan, that Duncan was still trying to persuade her to resume their relationship, that she was still angry with him and that he does not understand it. She told Ms Townsend that she had told her parents of the break up. All lies.

It is clear that these repeated dealings with Centacare placed Keli under considerable pressure. On 21 June 1995, Keli had an access visit to see Trisha and meet the proposed adoptive parents. Keli spoke to the parents about the reasons for wanting to adopt out Trisha. This added to Keli's stress.

Meanwhile, Keli's sporting activities had not abated. In January 1995, she represented New South Wales at an under-21's tournament in Perth, Western Australia. In April 1995, she was selected to compete in international water polo championships. On 2 July 1995, Keli journeyed to Canada to represent Australia in an under-20's water polo tournament. Keli returned to Australia on 14 July 1995, but she would never again initiate any contact with Centacare.

The adoption of Trisha would not be finalised until formal orders were made by the Supreme Court on 18 June 1996. The process had been, obviously enough, quite difficult for Keli. She would later tearfully describe having felt much hurt[5]. Also, it appears to me, she was quite perplexed by the process, in particular that it extended to swearing Supreme Court affidavits. Documents were being posted to her. This was not in keeping with her need to have the matter sorted quickly and secretly. Adoption was not the ideal solution for which Keli had hoped or anticipated.

Paul Roberts was not told of the birth or adoption of his child.

Fourth Pregnancy - Tegan

In December 1995 (before Trisha's adoption was finalised), Keli fell pregnant again. Based on dates, the Crown would later allege that 20 December was the likely date of conception[6]. I have seen other estimates that put the date of conception early in the new year of 1996. This was the pregnancy of which Tegan would be born.

Keli did not tell Duncan about the pregnancy. Nor, again, did he discern it. Because Tegan has never been found, there has never been DNA testing to ascertain paternity. Duncan would later maintain that he and Keli were having a full sexual relationship around the time of conception. By all accounts I have read, Duncan was an honest man and a reliable witness in court. Keli would later tell police there was no way the child was Duncan's child because she and Duncan had not had sexual relations for some time. There are accounts of Duncan being away during December 1995. However, on any view of these reports, he was in Sydney long enough to have had sexual relations with Keli, either in December 1995 or January 1996. Weighing all of this up, I am left with the impression that Duncan was probably the father of Tegan.

---

[5] *Exposed*, Episode 1 at 0.43, Episode 2 at 0.04.

[6] In Australia, the "Crown" is the term usually assigned to the prosecution. The prosecutor's title is "Crown Prosecutor". I shall in general use the term "Crown".

Also, in December 1995, Duncan purchased a house at 10 Venus Street, Gladesville. Keli would share her time between living there and living at her parents' place at Fairlight. Her parents did not become aware of the pregnancy.

In January 1996, Keli commenced studying at the Australian College of Physical Education ("ACPE"). Completion of these studies, if achieved, would earn her qualification as a physical education teacher.

In August 1996, Keli was eight months pregnant. She withdrew from the winter semester of study at ACPE. She signed a contract to undertake casual work as a water polo coach at Ravenswood School at Gordon in northern Sydney. This work was due to commence on 9 October. Keli also picked up work as a water polo coach at Wenona School for Girls at North Sydney. The Crown would later contend that these job commitments showed Keli had no intention of keeping her child who was due to be born in September.

Between Saturday 7 and Monday 9 September 1996, Duncan was away in the country on a football trip. The Crown's case would be that Keli seized this opportunity to try to have the birth of her child induced. On Saturday 7 September, Keli went to Ryde Hospital which was distant from Fairlight (about a 45 minute car journey in 1996) although it was reasonably close to Duncan's Gladesville address. She had never previously attended Ryde Hospital (or any hospital) in respect of her pregnancy. Keli told Ryde Hospital staff she wanted to have her baby induced. Keli told a number of lies to the hospital staff. She said she was booked in for a home birth with a private midwife, she lived at 70 Venus Street Gladesville (no such address existed), she was in transit from Perth and her partner was in the United Kingdom. Hospital staff considered she was only at week 38 of her pregnancy (two weeks early). The induction was refused.

On Tuesday 10 September 1996, Keli attended Ryde Hospital again. She told hospital staff she was two days over the 40 week mark of her pregnancy. More lies followed. She said she planned a home birth and that her home birth midwife was one Julie Melville. Ms Melville is Duncan's mother. She was not Keli's midwife. Nor did she know about Keli's pregnancy. An ultrasound at Ryde Hospital revealed no abnormality and Keli was discharged.

On Wednesday 11 September 1996, Keli attended Ryde Hospital again. And again hospital staff declined an induction. At 4.00pm on the same day, Keli attended Auburn Hospital which was even further away (in a westerly direction) from her local area. Auburn Hospital was about a 70 minute drive from Fairlight (and about 30 minutes from Duncan's place at Gladesville).

Keli told staff she was 12 days overdue. She gave the name of a friend, Kati Holt, as her contact person in case of emergency, but gave staff a phone number that was not in fact Ms Holt's phone number. Then followed another series of lies including that:

- her address was 70 Venus Avenue, Gladesville;
- all ante-natal care had been given by Julie Melville;
- she had been referred by Julie Melville to the hospital because she was overdue; and
- she had a miscarriage in Perth in 1994.

Keli was discharged that day with advice to return the following day for assessment and possible induction.

On Thursday 12 September 1996, Keli returned to Auburn Hospital. She rattled off more lies, however staff agreed to perform an induction.

It is worth noting there was no evidence of Keli undertaking any preparation for the birth. I have not found any evidence of attendance at birth classes. There was not even a single attendance on a medical practitioner. I am unaware of any evidence of Keli having acquired the normal accoutrements of childbirth, for example, cot, baby clothes or car baby capsule. No preparatory steps were taken for lawful adoption (there would later be evidence that usually mothers seeking adoption initiate the process prior to the birth).

Tegan Lee Lane was born just before 8.00pm. Staff were able to estimate from Tegan's physical condition that the pregnancy was only at the 38 week mark. Tegan was premature, but she was healthy. Keli had a severe haemorrhage with loss of one litre of blood. She was transferred to the maternity ward at 10.30pm. Nobody was with Keli during the birth or aftermath. Hospital staff saw no visitors, relatives, friends or support people attend Keli during her whole time at the hospital. Keli would later say, in a passing sort of way, that in fact she had received two visits. However, for reasons that will become obvious, this was almost certainly another fabrication.

Because Keli appeared to have no support, hospital staff arranged a consultation with a social worker, Ms Alicia Baltra-Vasquez, which took place on Friday 13 September 1996. Virtually everything said by Keli to Ms Baltra-Vasquez was false. Keli told her that:

- she had planned to have the baby at home with the assistance of an independent midwife;
- she had been born in Perth and her parents still lived there;
- she and her boyfriend had moved to Sydney a few months before;
- she had no family or friends in Sydney;
- it was intended that the boyfriend would be present at the birth but the birth was later than had been anticipated and he had football commitments overseas; and
- their plans were to move to London for a couple of years;

Ms Baltra-Vasquez observed Keli and Tegan together and thought *"it looked like the normal mother and things"* [sic]. Ms Baltra-Vasquez wrote in the hospital record that Keli was *"happy with her baby girl, breastfeeding her"*[7].

Keli told Ms Baltra-Vasquez that she planned to be discharged the next day (Saturday 14th) and that she would be able to manage at home. When told she might not be eligible for early discharge (because

---

[7] *Lane v. R* [2013] NSWCCA 317, at paragraph 193.

of lack of support), Keli came up with a support network second to none. A throng of people would be turning up: her boyfriend would be returning from overseas, her parents would be coming over from Perth, a "*lady*" was dropping in to stay until her parents arrived and her own midwife, Julie Melville, would be making regular home visits.

On the morning of Saturday 14 September, Keli told nursing staff she was keen to be discharged as soon as possible. There were several matters which required attention before discharge. Some of these matters were attended to, and some were not. Tegan was examined by a doctor. Keli signed a form which authorised the addition of Tegan's name to her Medicare card. In addition, arrangements were made for Keli to be visited at home by a midwife from the Ryde Domiciliary Midwife Program ("RDMP"). A birth registration form was given to Keli to complete and submit to the Registry of Births Deaths and Marriages. A Guthrie test was supposed to be done[8]. There was also an identification procedure that was supposed to be undertaken.

Keli discharged herself, with Tegan, at some stage between 11.00am and 12.00 midday. There were different routes out of the hospital. It was not known by which route she departed. None of the nursing staff observed her leave, or knew she had left. She did not submit Tegan for identification checks as had been requested of her. No Guthrie test had been performed[9].

Later that day, at about 3.00pm, Keli arrived at her parents' home at Fairlight. Tegan was not with her. Keli's parents remained completely unaware of the pregnancy or Tegan's birth. Duncan also remained unaware.

Precisely how Keli got from Auburn Hospital to Fairlight is not known. Keli had a car and the likelihood was that she drove herself from the hospital. (Amongst other things, she entered her parents' home through the back door, which was consistent with her having arrived at the premises by car.) To my knowledge, Keli has never

---

[8] A Guthrie test is a heel prick blood test designed to detect genetic conditions. Being a blood test, it is also capable of being used for DNA testing.

[9] There would never be any DNA testing from which Tegan's paternity could be ascertained. As mentioned previously, the probability was that Duncan was in fact the father, but this has never been able to be scientifically confirmed.

explained why it took at least three, possibly four, hours to get from Auburn to Fairlight.

Duncan arrived at Fairlight separately from Keli, but at about the same time. At about 4.00pm, Keli's mother drove Keli and Duncan to attend the wedding of an acquaintance of Duncan. Video of that wedding showed Keli and revealed nothing untoward. Keli appeared composed, with sunglasses atop her head. Keli mentioned nothing of Tegan's birth to anybody. The judge who would later preside over Keli's trial, Justice Anthony Whealy ("Whealy J"), would say that the "*oral evidence . . . suggested*" that Keli was "*quieter than usual*" at the wedding and that she "*went home early*"[10]. However, there was also evidence that Keli appeared her normal self, socialising, drinking and dancing.

On Monday 16 September 1996, Keli telephoned RDMP and advised she would not be needing a domiciliary midwife. Keli said her "*home birth midwife*" would be taking over care of Tegan and herself. No midwife ever contacted Auburn Hospital, as would have been expected.

On Thursday 19 September 1996, Tegan became enrolled on Keli's Medicare card. By the time of Keli's trial in 2010, no rebate had ever been claimed from Medicare in respect of Tegan. Nor had Tegan's birth been registered – that would not happen until a Coroner made an order for registration of Tegan's birth in 2005. Nor could any record be found of Tegan having attended a school.

Curiously, there was not a single withdrawal from Keli's Westpac bank account between May and October 1996. To my knowledge, Keli has never spoken about this. It has generated rumours to the effect that she sold Tegan in a surrogacy deal. However, there might be several explanations for the inactivity on Keli's bank account. For example, she might have had another account that she used (police were unable to obtain warrants to search other banks). Or perhaps she was sustained on cash handouts from her parents. This draws support from evidence

---

[10] *R v. Lane* [2011] NSWSC 289 at paragraph 13.

given by her father at an inquest in 2005[11]. If there was a surrogacy deal, it might be expected that Keli would say so, especially when, as will be seen, she would later be offered an immunity from prosecution for "coming clean" about what happened to Tegan. But Keli has said nothing about a surrogacy deal. I consider it is almost certain there was no such deal.

In October 1996, Keli commenced her employment as the water polo coach at Ravenswood School and it appears she was well able to perform her teaching duties. She did not continue her course at ACPE.

Between 1996 and 1998, Keli's water polo aspirations were on a roller coaster. There was increasing talk of women's water polo being included in the 2000 Olympic Games. In 1997 Keli was a member of the New South Wales senior team. Also, in 1997, her club team Balmain won the Sydney women's water polo premiership. In October, it was announced that water polo would be included in the Sydney Olympics. But Keli's hopes were dashed when she was dropped from the state team. She also missed national selection for the Women's World Cup. None of this seems to have deterred Keli. In 1997, she wrote to ACPE asking for a year and a half away from studies to concentrate on making the national squad. And in February 1998, Keli wrote to ACPE requesting that her practical teaching scheduled for that month be deferred because she wanted to focus on selection for the Sydney Olympics.

Fifth Pregnancy

Keli and Duncan separated in March 1998. In August 1998, Keli found herself pregnant again. Later DNA testing would reveal that a man named Alan Howard was the father. Mr Howard was a friend of Keli's brother (Morgan). Keli did not tell Mr Howard of the pregnancy and, again, no family or friends knew of it.

It is appropriate at this juncture to deal with the enduring question of how nobody close to Keli realised she was pregnant through three

---

[11] See also Langdon, A., *The Child Who Never Was*, Park Street Press, 2007, at pp. 71 to 72.

full term pregnancies. It seems counter-intuitive. It has given rise to a myriad of theories and suspicions about whether people really knew, whether "the parents know more than they're letting on", whether somebody's involvement was being "covered up" and even, incredibly, whether incest was involved.

In court cases, counter-intuitive things pop up from time to time. Sometimes the evidence trumps intuition, sometimes it does not. In this case, it seems to me, the evidence was overwhelming that in truth nobody recognised Keli was pregnant and there was nothing sinister about this. The evidence can be summarised as follows:

1. Most of those close to Keli, including her parents and Duncan, testified more than once in court. By all accounts, all were reliable witnesses who were candid in their evidence. They denied knowing about any of the pregnancies. For this reason alone, it is almost certain that nobody close to Keli actually recognised the pregnancies;

2. The evidence in favour of the pregnancies being detectable was slight, almost to the point of non-existent. The only evidence I have seen or heard came from fellow water polo players who said they suspected pregnancy when they went underwater and saw Keli's abdomen. I have not seen any evidence that Keli's parents or Duncan participated in these water polo games (or training), nor that the other players reported their observations to any Lane family member or Duncan;

3. Keli's weight was known to go up and down frequently, leading to the inference that any suspicion of pregnancy could reasonably have been dismissed as just Keli's normal weight gain;

4. Keli's mum has stated that Keli wore baggy clothes, doubtless to assist with keeping the pregnancies secret. I have not seen any evidence to contradict Keli's mum. Therefore, it can be safely accepted that Keli probably

wore baggy clothes and succeeded in camouflaging her pregnancies; and

5. There was the overarching circumstance that Keli was very determined to hide her pregnancies. We have seen that she went to great lengths, even heading off mail at a Post Office. Of itself, this might not mean she ultimately succeeded in her endeavours, but it does generate additional comfort about accepting the evidence of the parents and Duncan.

For these reasons, in my opinion, this is a case where the evidence comfortably prevails over intuition and it can be safely assumed nobody close to Keli ever did realise she was pregnant.

In February 1999, Keli travelled to Brisbane to attend an abortion clinic and seek a termination but was told by the clinic staff that it was too late. She told the clinic staff a number of untruths, including that she was already a mother. She gave staff a wrong phone number.

On 31 May 1999, Keli delivered a healthy child who she named Archie. This delivery took place at Ryde Hospital. Keli had told a plethora of lies to the staff at Ryde Hospital on a pre-confinement admission (21 May). On delivery of Archie she told more lies:

- she had delivered and breastfed a child in 1996 (breastfeeding for six months); and
- the child was well;

On 1 June 1999, whilst still in hospital, Keli contacted Anglicare Adoption Services for the purpose of surrendering Archie to adoption. She falsely told Anglicare staff she had travelled from London to have the baby in Sydney and that she had counselling in England. Keli then came under the care of an Anglicare social worker by the name of Virginia Fung for completion of the adoption process. Mr Howard was not told of the birth or proposed adoption of his child.

Keli told Ms Fung the following:

- she was due to start work in London in the middle of June;
- her ex-partner Duncan was the father of Archie and he was in London;
- Duncan had left her when she was five months pregnant;
- Duncan knew about Archie's birth;
- she had discussed adoption with Duncan and did not believe he was interested in parenting Archie; and
- she had not lived with her parents since she was 17 years old.

None of this was true.

On 2 June 1999 Keli was discharged from Ryde Hospital, leaving Archie for adoption. Archie was placed into foster care while awaiting adoption. Ms Fung told Keli that Duncan's consent was needed or else the process might be long and difficult, something Keli would have known in any event.

During the ensuing weeks, Keli told Ms Fung lie after lie, for example:

- she had been living with Duncan in London since June 1998;
- Duncan had a football contract in London;
- Duncan had frozen their joint bank account in London, leaving her without funds;
- she had been in contact with her employer in England who had allowed her to remain in Australia until mid-July;
- she hoped her mother would come out from England to accompany her on the return journey to London;
- she was staying with a friend at 10 Venus Street, Gladesville;
- the other people at 10 Venus Street may not have seen her before admission to hospital and therefore may not know she was living there;
- she was having trouble with her visa for re-entry to the UK and may have to go to Canberra to sort it out; and
- she was due back in London on 12 July to start a work contract with a school.

During June 1999, Ms Fung found it increasingly difficult to contact Keli. All of the contact numbers supplied by Keli were found to be wrong numbers and Keli's mobile phone was usually turned off. Ms Fung went to 10 Venus Street looking for Keli but the occupants of the house did not know her.

Having been unable to contact Keli, Ms Fung referred the matter to the Department of Community Services ("DOCS") because she was unsure of Archie's legal status and the foster care agreement was about to expire.

The DOCS officer to whom the case was assigned was a Mr John Borovnik. In the course of his normal enquiries he happened upon the fact that Keli had presented to Ryde Hospital in the late stages of a pregnancy in 1996. He communicated this to Ms Fung.

On 7 July 1999, Keli attended Ms Fung's office and told her that Archie was her first child. Ms Fung quizzed her about having a baby in 1996. Keli said that it was her friend Lisa Andreatta who had a child in 1996. The following week, Keli told Ms Fung that if anybody from Anglicare was going to contact Duncan they should not mention the adoption. She also said she would provide Duncan's phone number.

In a last-ditch effort to find Duncan, Ms Fung wrote a letter to him and posted it to Manly Rugby Club. Ms Fung asked Duncan to contact her in regard to Keli and attached photographs of Keli and baby Archie together at Ryde Hospital. Manly Rugby Club forwarded the letter to Duncan's last known address at 10 Venus Street where it was opened by one of the residents, Clayton Baldwin, who knew Duncan and gave him the letter[12].

On 27 July 1999, a doubtless bewildered Duncan confronted Keli about Ms Fung's letter. Keli denied there was a baby, but then said there was a baby but he was not supposed to know about it. Eventually, Keli conceded to Duncan that he was not the father of

---

[12] Duncan no longer owned 10 Venus Street, having sold it to his brother Simon, who had rented it out to Clayton Baldwin. Clayton knew both of the Gillies brothers.

Archie. Duncan told Ms Fung that he was definitely not the father. Keli conceded to Ms Fung that Duncan was not the father.

Troubled by this turn of events, and whether Keli was in a fit state of mind to make a decision about adopting out Archie, Ms Fung arranged for Keli to be seen by a psychiatrist, Dr Debra Montgomery. This appointment was scheduled for 6 September 1999. Meanwhile, on 1 September, Keli met with Ms Fung and offered a new explanation to the effect that a person called "Aaron Williams" was Archie's father. Keli stated that "Aaron Williams" was an Australian living in London and working in the computer section of Barclays Bank in north London.

On 6 September 1999, Keli attended the appointment with Dr Montgomery. Dr Montgomery found Keli was not cognitively impaired and was able to form a judgment about the adoption.

On 7 September 1999, Ms Fung telephoned the Sydney and London offices of Barclays Bank and was told the bank had no record of an "Aaron Williams" being employed.

On 13 September 1999, Keli swore an affidavit for the purposes of Archie's adoption proceedings. She stated the following in the affidavit:

- the father of Archie was "Aaron Williams";
- she had met "Aaron Williams" in London, where they both resided and where she fell pregnant to him;
- "Aaron Williams" had a university degree and worked at Barclay's Bank in London
- she was unable to contact "Aaron Williams" or provide any contact details for him; and
- when she told "Aaron Williams" she was pregnant he consented to the adoption out of Archie and she had no further contact with him.

All of these statements were false. As previously mentioned, the father of Archie was in fact Alan Howard who would later state that he had a four to six month relationship with Keli around the time of Archie's conception. The false statements about "Aaron Williams" would later give rise to a third charge of false swearing. There was, of course, no such person as "Aaron Williams".

Meanwhile, at DOCS, Mr Borovnik had continued his enquiries and discovered that Keli had indeed delivered a baby in 1996. On 18 October 1999, he rang Keli and asked her if she had given birth to a child at Auburn Hospital in 1996. Keli denied she had done so. Mr Borovnik asked if she was sure and Keli said she was. She said she was not pregnant in 1996. She also denied she had attended Ryde Hospital in a pregnant condition in 1996. Mr Borovnik suspected foul play and told Keli he would have to pass the information on to the police.

On Wednesday 20 October 1999, Keli sent the following fax to Mr Borovnik:

> *"I will be speaking to Virginia Fung to discuss those facts. Many people have been involved who actually have no knowledge of what's occurred. Therefore, in your inquiry please do not contact them before giving me prior notice as they will be completely unaware of what you are talking about. I suggest you contact Virginia Fung after Monday to confirm the facts"*

On Monday 25 October 1999, Keli wrote a letter to Ms Fung that read, in part:

> *"Firstly, thank you for all of your time, your patience and your understanding even though I have not been entirely honest with you. I'm glad now that I can stop telling half truths and lies and perhaps move on in my life. You are the first person in a long time who has reached out to help me without me feeling like I was being judged. It must be very hard for you to understand what has been going on and why I have done the things I've done and I'm not sure I can give you all the answers. Over all of these weeks my main concern was [Archie] and making sure that*

he was safe and happy and that you would find him a loving and secure home.

So where do I start? I'm not sure? My life for the last 6 years has been a nightmare . . . . Many people, including my family, have disowned me and looking at the situation I guess it's not hard to figure out why. There were 3 children obviously I can't lie anymore as the paperwork is there. The middle child lives with a family in Perth although I have not had contact with them for a long time. They befriended me just before I had her and supported us . . ."

Despite the contrition expressed in the opening sentence, and the vow to stop lying in the second sentence, the letter contained more lies. In particular, Keli's family had never disowned her and the middle child (Tegan) was not with a family in Perth.

On 4 November 1999, Mr Borovnik (DOCS) made his report to police. In late November, the matter was assigned to Detective Senior Constable Mathew Kehoe (hereafter "Kehoe") at Manly Police Station. Unfortunately, the investigation proceeded at a glacial pace. It would not be until 14 February 2001 that Keli was formally interviewed by Kehoe[13].

Meanwhile, on 30 June 2000, the Supreme Court made an order formalising the adoption of Archie. By this time, Keli had commenced living in a de facto relationship with a man named Peter Cains. In about August 2000, Keli was pregnant again. Mr Cains was the father.

---

[13] I have found it difficult to pin down the reason/s for the delay. There are some accounts of Kehoe being over-worked and under-resourced and another account of him being on leave. It also appears he was absent from work for lengthy periods due to attendance at an enquiry into the conduct of certain officers at Manly police station. There was no suggestion that Kehoe himself was the subject of enquiry or a "person of interest". The New South Wales State Coroner, Mr John Abernethy, did not call Kehoe as a witness at an inquest held in 2005/06 although he did comment: *"I can only say that [the delay] made the ongoing investigation into the disappearance of Tegan Lane incredibly difficult".* He criticised the police service for applying insufficient resources to the investigation. I have requested an explanation for the delay from the Commissioner of Police. The Commissioner has told me the matter has been referred to the appropriate area of the police force and a reply will be forthcoming. As at the date of this book going into print, I have not received a reply.

2001 – Interview with Detective Mathew Kehoe[14]

The interview on 14 February 2001 proceeded in a peculiar way. It consisted almost entirely of Kehoe putting leading questions to Keli. A leading question is one that suggests its own answer. There is not anything necessarily wrong with putting leading questions in an interview, although it would normally be wise to minimise them.

The most notable matter revealed in the interview was that Keli claimed to have given Tegan to a man named "Andrew Morris", who she maintained was Tegan's natural father. Keli alleged she had first met "Andrew" in December 1995. She claimed to have had a brief affair with him and believed he was about 30 years old. She stated she had arranged with "Andrew" that he (with his girlfriend "Mel") would take custody of Tegan because she, Keli, was unable to care for her. Keli made no mention of "Andrew" requesting a paternity test to confirm he was the natural father. There has never been any evidence of a paternity test having been performed. The arrangement was that "Andrew" would come to the hospital and collect Tegan. According to Keli, "Andrew" and his mother, and "Mel", visited Keli twice at the hospital[15]. Keli said she left the hospital "*before 12 o'clock sometime*" on Saturday 14 September 1996, and "Andrew" "*dropped me home and then took Tegan with him*".

This was Keli's first mention of a person named "Andrew Morris" (or "Mel") and the "*arrangement*" in respect of Tegan. She had not mentioned any of this back in 1999 to the staff at Ryde Hospital (in discussions about the baby born in 1996) or to Mr Borovnik or Ms Fung. Nor had Keli mentioned "Andrew Morris" to anybody at Auburn or Ryde Hospitals in 1996. Indeed, prior to conjuring up the throng of support people that would be at her home after Tegan's birth, Keli had maintained she had no friends or family in Sydney, implying she had no support people, which was inconsistent with the notion that

---

[14] Record of interview 14 February 2001.

[15] It will be recalled that none of the medical or nursing staff saw anybody visit Keli.

somebody was coming to take Tegan. There were other puzzling features about Keli's story. For example, why had she told the RDMP (on 16 September 1996) that her "*home birth midwife*" would be taking over the care of herself and Tegan if in fact "Andrew" was taking over the care of Tegan ? Why had she told Ryde Hospital staff (in 1999) that she breastfed the baby born in 1996 for six months if in fact "Andrew" had taken over the care of that baby ? How, in 1999, was she able to tell Ryde Hospital staff that the baby born in 1996 was well if she hadn't seen it or heard from "Andrew" for some three years or so?

Keli told Kehoe that she did not know where "Andrew Morris" was, but that he had previously lived in Balmain. When Kehoe asked Keli if she would be able to identify the Balmain residence of "Andrew Morris", Keli answered: "*No, I'm not able to do that*". This answer was somewhat baffling. Many years later Keli was able to tell an *Exposed* reporter that the residence was only a two minute walk from the pub where she met "Andrew" which suggests it would not have been too hard to locate.

By the time of Kehoe's interview in 2001, it was 16 months since the phone conversation with Mr Borovnik and there was no sign of Keli herself having done anything to ascertain what was happening in respect of Tegan. For all that was known by Keli, "Andrew" and Tegan might still have been in Balmain and able to be located (if they existed). Indeed, the question arises as to why Keli did not seek out "Andrew" and Tegan back in 1999 when she first came on notice that there was an issue about Tegan's whereabouts serious enough to warrant notification of the police.

Keli told Kehoe that "Andrew's" mobile phone might still be connected and she would "*start looking tonight . . . most of my things are packed up so it's just a matter of going through things*".

2002 – Interview with Detective Richard Gaut

After the Kehoe interview, for reasons that remain obscure, the police investigation ground to a halt. In October 2002, Detective Richard

Gaut ("Gaut") took over the then dormant investigation. On 16 October, Gaut had a discussion with Keli that was not video recorded. The conversation was to this effect:

> Gaut: *So Keli, we need to find Tegan, what are the circumstances of who you gave the child to and how it was given over?*
> Keli: *Yes, I gave her to her father, a man named Andrew Norris.*
>
> Gaut: *You told Detective Kehoe his name was Morris*
> Keli: *No I told him Norris*
>
> Gaut: *OK so two days after Tegan was born you were discharged from the hospital. You met the father Andrew outside, got into his car and he drove you and Tegan to Duncan's place in Gladesville*
> Keli: *No that's not what happened*
>
> Gaut: *Well what did happen?*
> Keli: *Andrew Norris was furious when I told him I was pregnant. He called me a slut. But he and Mel wanted to raise the baby. I left the hospital and Andrew, Mel and Andrew's mum were outside. They took Tegan from me in the car park and left me to catch a taxi home.*
>
> Gaut: *Keli this is a very different story to what you told Detective Kehoe a year or so ago. You told Detective Kehoe that Andrew, with his partner and his mother, had driven you to Gladesville.*
> Keli: *Well I lied to him because I was embarrassed about Andrew hating me. I told him that because that's what I wanted to happen. I felt like a slut. I wanted to make it sound better, the fact that they didn't care about me.*

Gaut: *And you have absolutely no idea where Andrew or Tegan are? In fact none of your friends have heard of Andrew Norris have they?*

Keli: *There was a lot of people I used to hang around back then who aren't in my life now. My friend Lisa Andreatta knew him. Lisa's in Brisbane. She knew Andrew and Mel. She also knew I had an affair with him behind Mel's back.*

Gaut: *Does your friend know about Tegan's birth ?*
Keli: *Yes*

Gaut: *Can you please give me Lisa's details ?*
Keli: *Ah no, I can't. We lost touch over the last few years. I don't know where she is or what she's doing these days.*

Gaut: *Well could you find the apartment where Andrew lived when you were seeing each other? I need that address.*
Keli: *I'll try.*

Gaut: *Can you give a description of Andrew Norris?*
Keli: *He'd now be about 36 years old, bleached blonde hair, well built , tanned, worked in finance or banking, I think he attended Sydney University.*

And so Keli's story had changed markedly. Now the surname of "Andrew" was "Norris" rather than "Morris". And whereas she told Kehoe that "*[Andrew] dropped me home and then took Tegan*", she now told Gaut that "*Andrew, Mel and Andrew's mum . . . took Tegan from me in the [hospital] car park and left me to catch a taxi home*". This was the second (different) version of the hand-over of Tegan, with Keli admitting the first was a lie. The only other occasion on which Keli has (publicly) explained the hand-over was when interviewed on *Exposed* when she stated that it occurred in a foyer area of the hospital[16]. This was the third different version.

Apart from the inconsistencies, there were implausibilities about each version of the hand-over. It was improbable that a man in his thirties would, with his partner, take over the care of a baby born out of an affair. It was even more improbable when, according to information later given by Keli, it was something about which he felt "*so much embarrassment*", and so trapped and unhappy, he did not even know how he could stay in Sydney[17]. And all of this without as much as a question about a paternity test. It was equally improbable that "Mel" would accept this responsibility in circumstances where the baby was born of an affair behind her back <u>and</u> she hated Keli[18] <u>and</u> she would do so without questioning paternity <u>and</u> she would presumably also have to uproot her life by leaving Sydney.

Another implausible feature of Keli's story was that she would give Tegan to the alleged natural father ("Andrew") in circumstances where she fabricated the details of the natural fathers of the other two unwanted children, Trisha and Archie. These fabrications were, plainly enough, designed with an eye to eliminating the possibility of the real natural fathers ever turning up on Keli's door step. This was one of Keli's ways of ensuring the adoptions became permanent. In this circumstance, it tends to defy belief that Keli would give Tegan to her (alleged) real natural father "Andrew" and run the risk of him showing up at a later stage. Handing Tegan to "Andrew" was not a permanent solution at all. It can be inferred from this, in my view, that in truth Keli never did hand Tegan to "Andrew".

Finally, to confound things even further, Keli told *Exposed* in 2018 that maybe "Andrew" was lying about his name or maybe she was mistaken.

---

[16] *Exposed*, Episode 3, at 0.30ff.

[17] Interview with Gaut on 9 May 2003.

[18] Interview with Gaut on 8 January 2004.

It might be inferred that Keli gave her two day old baby to a person whose surname she did not know. When this is married up with the apparent reluctance of "Andrew", the situation is quite unreal. On one view of it, Keli's story has become that she gave her two day old baby to a person:

(1) whose partner hated her;
(2) whose surname she did not know; and
(3) who was so *"embarrassed"*, and feeling so trapped and unhappy about taking Tegan, that he might have to leave Sydney, but who nevertheless did not require a paternity test.

It is hard to conclude other than that the story about handing Tegan over to "Andrew Morris/Norris" was a concoction.

After the 16 October interview, Gaut's enquiries continued and he discovered Keli was lying about Lisa Andreatta's knowledge of "Andrew". Lisa told Gaut she knew nothing of him. And Lisa had never lived in Brisbane.

Then followed a telling sequence of events. On 17 October 2002, Keli informed Gaut that she would go to 10 Venus Street, Gladesville and try to locate old diaries containing telephone numbers of friends who could verify the existence of "Andrew Norris". On Thursday 7 November, not having heard from Keli, Gaut phoned to see how she was going with locating the diaries. Keli said she was intending to visit 10 Venus Street on Saturday 9 November. She also said she had otherwise been unable to find numbers for anybody who had known of "Andrew Norris". There followed a series of unsuccessful attempts by Gaut to phone Keli. It was plain to see that Keli was avoiding Gaut[19]. On 2 December, Gaut went to 10 Venus Street and spoke to two of the residents then living there. They said nobody had turned up to search for old papers.

---

[19] *Lane v. R* [2013] NSWCCA 317, at paragraph 221.

2003 – Second interview with Detective Gaut

On 9 May 2003, Gaut interviewed Keli at Manly police station. This interview was wide ranging and probing. Gaut asked Keli about her fax to Ms Fung in which she stated that "*the middle child*" (Tegan) lived with a family in Perth. She told Gaut she was not sure what "Andrew" was going to do, conveying the impression that he was (part of) the family in Perth. She then stated that she took from some of her conversations with "Andrew" that he was not going to stay in Sydney because of "*embarrassment*". She claimed "Andrew" had said "*I don't know how I could stay in Sydney, what will everyone think, it's such an embarrassment*".

Then followed more obfuscation by Keli as she tried to dilute the significance of her fax to Ms Fung. Keli asked "*Was there more to the letter? I trusted Virginia a lot. This fax comes from the end of a conversation we had when she visited me at work. It's not very detailed because we'd already had the conversation*". This tactic failed as Gaut pressed on regardless: "*Why wouldn't you just tell her Tegan is with Andrew, her father?*". Keli was now forced to make things up on the run: "*I think in one conversation I did tell her that Tegan was living with her father. Perhaps you should speak with Virginia*". But Gaut was one step ahead of Keli: "*I've spoken with Virginia. Don't you agree that this fax doesn't read as if Tegan is with her father? That it reads as though she is with some couple that you've met and who have befriended you?*". Keli's responses began to sound rattled: "*I didn't give her away to anybody! That's what you are trying to say it says and it doesn't*" [sic]. Keli was now cornered and her story collapsed into an assertion that the reference to the Perth family in the fax was in fact a reference to "Andrew" and "Mel". Keli then confirmed she had never before mentioned that "Andrew" and "Mel" were from Perth. She was unable to say why she had not done so.

Gaut told Keli that Tegan's birth had never been registered, no Medicare claim had ever been made in respect of Tegan and no school authority had any record of Tegan's enrolment. Keli was evasive. She had no satisfactory explanation for any of these matters.

Gaut revealed he had spoken to Lisa Andreatta and that she knew nothing of an "Andrew Norris". Keli said she thought Lisa knew "Andrew" because she was there when "Andrew" was around. There was no reply by Keli when Gaut asked if there was anybody else who might know about her relationship with "Andrew Norris".

Gaut then asked Keli about the searches she was going to undertake through old boxes at 10 Venus Street, Gladesville. Gaut had spoken to the tenants who denied anybody had been there searching for papers. Keli claimed the tenants denied her access.

Gaut then confronted Keli about being truthful. He told her that now was the opportunity to tell the truth and asked if there was anything else she wanted to say. Then followed 50 seconds of silence. Gaut repeated the question and there was another 14 seconds of silence. Gaut asked Keli if she killed Tegan and Keli loudly denied she had done so. Keli asked for the tape to be stopped. Gaut said he preferred to keep the tape going. Keli responded: *"OK I don't understand how you're gonna go and speak with my parents or people like that who have no idea what you're talking about. This is between me and Andrew. [inaudible] He told me not to connect him".* The last sentence was presumably a reference to "Andrew" not being connected, although this was puzzling given that Keli had freely offered up his name at the interview with Kehoe and had not been reluctant to connect him in discussions with either Kehoe or Gaut. Perhaps the identity of the person who told Keli he did not want to be "connected" will never be known. Or perhaps nobody had said that they did not want to be connected.

There was then the following exchange between Gaut and Keli:

> Gaut: *Do you understand the information you've given me, right, I'm very open minded, very reasonable, but the information you've given me makes me highly suspicious that something has happened to the child.*

> Keli: *Nothing has happened to her. Nothing has happened to her. He said he would contact me if there was an emergency. I have not heard cooee from them, not one word. I don't have anything else to say.*

Drive Around Balmain with Detective Gaut

On 19 May 2003, Keli accompanied Gaut on a drive around Balmain in an effort to identify the apartment block where "Andrew" had lived. It will be recalled Keli had previously (in 2002) told Gaut she would try to find the block. In 2001, she had told Kehoe she was "*not able*" to point out "Andrew's" address. This was notwithstanding that the block was, according to information later given by Keli to *Exposed*, less than a two minute walk from the pub where she first met him[20]. At any rate, after driving around Balmain with Gaut for about 10 minutes, Keli identified a block of apartments at 24 Wisbeach Street Balmain (hereafter "Wisbeach"). Gaut and Keli entered the block and Keli identified the units numbered 10 or 11 as "Andrew's" place.

By the time of Keli's identification of Wisbeach to Gaut, it was over three years since she had spoken to Mr Borovnik and over two years since she had spoken to Kehoe and yet this was evidently the first time she had tried to find "Andrew's" residence. This was mysterious, to say the least. As discussed, if "Andrew" existed, and lived at Wisbeach with Tegan, they might have still been there in 1999, or in the years intervening.

The occupant of unit 10 at Wisbeach at the relevant time (late 1995/early 1996) was identified as a Mr Sean Greaves. He was located and interviewed. Mr Greaves had never used the name "Andrew Morris" or "Andrew Norris", and he knew nobody by either name. Mr Greaves did not recall receiving mail for anybody by those names. He denied having a woman called "Mel" stay in his unit.

---

[20] *Exposed*, Episode 2, 0.26.

Peter Clark lived at unit 11 with his brother Steven between December 1995 and December 1996. Mr Clark said he knew a man by the name of Andrew Morris who had occasionally visited him, but he was of partly Asian appearance and did not fit the description of the "Andrew Morris" alleged by Keli. The police interviewed this Andrew Morris and he definitely was not the father of Tegan. He had not taken possession of a baby called Tegan from Auburn Hospital.

Mr Clark also claimed he had seen mail addressed to each of "Andrew Morris" and "Andrew Norris" sitting on top of the mail box for unit 10 (Mr Greaves' unit). However, Mr Clark's evidence would ultimately prove to be *"of dubious (if any) reliability"* for reasons that will be discussed in a later chapter[21]. It can be safely assumed there was no mail addressed to "Andrew Morris" or "Andrew Norris" found by Mr Clark at Wisbeach.

During the rest of 2003, Gaut continued searching for "Andrew Norris" and Tegan with no success.

2004 – Third interview with Detective Gaut

On 8 January 2004, Gaut interviewed Keli again at Manly police station. Keli told Gaut she discovered she was pregnant with Tegan in March or April 1996 and she had informed "Andrew Norris" in about May. "Andrew" had asked Keli if she was going to get rid of the baby. She replied it was too late and wanted to know if he would take it. Keli said "Andrew" wasn't too happy about it. Keli said "Andrew" was rude, aggressive and not pleased, and that he had accused her of trapping him and being a slut. After that, Keli told Gaut, there was no contact with "Andrew" until she called him from the hospital the day after Tegan was born (which would have been Friday 13 September). Gaut asked Keli about "Mel" and Keli said that "Mel" hated her, but was nonetheless happy to take Tegan. Keli agreed this was odd.

---

[21] *Lane v. R* [2013] NSWCCA 317, at paragraph 252, see also paragraphs 144 to 169.

2004 – First Coronial Inquest

In August 2004, an inquest into the disappearance of Tegan under the *Coroner's Act 1980* (NSW) was held. The presiding Coroner was Mr Carl Milovanovich. A non-publication order was made. The proceeding was held in a closed court. Mr Milovanovich offered Keli an immunity "deal". The precise terms of the deal are not available. The terms were reported by *Exposed* as being to the effect that Keli would be given an immunity from prosecution in exchange for "coming clean" about Tegan. In an interview on *Exposed*, Mr Milovanovich emphasised that the immunity did not extend to cover murder charges. Although I have not seen its terms, I am content for present purposes to assume that an immunity deal was offered but it did not extend to cover liability for murder.

Keli rejected the immunity deal and invitation to "come clean". She explained this to *Exposed* by saying she was not prepared to state things in evidence that were not correct and she was not going to admit to something she did not do. In other words, she was sticking to her story of giving Tegan to "Andrew Norris". It is tempting to think that Keli's rejection of the immunity deal was an indication that she truly believed in the version she had proffered (of giving Tegan to "Andrew"). And this seems to have been the way it was taken by the *Exposed* interviewer who exclaimed:

> *"So you never entertained taking, wow, even when it would have meant you wouldn't have spent a day in gaol"*[22] [sic]

However, it is not clear to me that the inference apparently drawn by the reporter was available. There was no immunity for murder. No matter what evidence Keli might have given before the Coroner, she remained exposed to a murder prosecution (and of course imprisonment if found guilty). Indeed, there was a real risk it would

---

[22] *Exposed*, Episode 2, at 0.47.

be harmful to Keli's interests because it would entail Keli giving sworn evidence. With Keli's history of deceit, it was probably best for her to avoid giving evidence. Even if I am incorrect, the notion that the strength of a person's belief in their own innocence is objectively probative of their innocence, which is what I understood the *Exposed* reporter was seeking to convey, is misconceived.

2005 – Second Coronial Inquest

On 20 June 2005, another inquest was commenced, this time before the New South Wales State Coroner, Mr John Abernethy (hereafter "the Coroner"). Keli elected not to give evidence, as was her right. Most of Keli's known friends gave evidence. Each testified that they had no knowledge of anybody resembling "Andrew Morris/Norris".

On 23 June 2005, the Coroner issued his own appeal to the Australian public for information: "*I'd simply make the appeal at this stage of this inquest, if there is a couple out there, be they from New South Wales or elsewhere . . . who has this child without the child being legally adopted, this is their opportunity to come forward and give that information to either an adoption agency or preferably the officer-in-charge of this case*". Evidence was given by a Ms Candlin from Centacare to the effect that the illegality of the adoption could be overcome simply by Keli signing an adoption consent. Ms Candlin testified that discretion was assured to the adoptive parents and Tegan. Still, nobody came forward.

On 27 June 2005, the Coroner issued another plea, this time to people who may have known a childless couple who had a child suddenly appear. There was no response.

In his closing submissions, Keli's counsel, Peter Hamill SC, conceded that Keli had been deceitful but denied she had committed any crime. This concession set the tone of the defence that Keli would run through until the end of her trial. That is to say, Keli would always, in essence, concede she had an extraordinary history of deceiving people, but deny murdering Tegan.

In his findings delivered on 15 February 2006, the Coroner highlighted the difficulty facing the police in their searches for "Andrew" and Tegan, in particular that they were trying to prove a negative, i.e. that Tegan was not dead. He also acknowledged the difficulty created for the police by the lies and inconsistencies in Keli's story. He commented that it was impossible for Gaut to follow up leads because he could never tell if Keli was telling the truth or not.

Ultimately, the Coroner was unsatisfied with Keli's explanation about handing Tegan over to "Andrew Norris" and he considered Keli was evasive and had told a *"litany of lies"*. He found he could not accept any truth in the story about "Andrew Norris" and he was *"completely unable to accept the final version given by [Keli]"*:

> *"I have to say that I find it inherently unlikely that a man with whom she was having an affair, already had a partner, who initially at least was incredibly angry on learning she was pregnant, nevertheless was happy to take the child"*

The Coroner was comfortably satisfied that Tegan was deceased but considered there was insufficient evidence to lay charges against Keli. He found Tegan had died in 1996, probably in the days following her birth, but was unable to assign a place, manner or cause of the death. He referred the matter to the New South Wales Homicide Squad for further investigation.

The Search Continues

Between 2006 and 2008, searches continued for "Andrew Morris/ Norris" and Tegan. These searches were enormous. They covered every imaginable record and organisation, for example Registry of Births, Deaths and Marriages (more than 12,000 births investigated), electoral rolls,

University of Sydney, New South Wales Water Polo Organisation, various water polo clubs, Roads and Traffic Authority, Centrelink, Australia Post, Department of Fair Trading, missing persons records, Department of Immigration, telephone and electricity records and education authorities throughout Australia. Many of these searches were undertaken not just once, but repeatedly. Extensive investigations were undertaken of the Wisbeach apartments. More than 86,000 births in NSW between 31 March 1996 and 30 September 1997 were cross-checked against hospital records. Forty one men by the name of Andrew Norris or Morris were identified with birth dates between 1960 and 1976. Statements were taken from each man that could be located. And so on.

The investigation revealed that nobody had used the form given by the Auburn Hospital staff to Keli to register Tegan's birth. No adoption agency in Australia had records of an adoption of Tegan. Checks were made of all babies named Tegan born in September 1996 and cross-checks were made against various surnames and parental names, including "Morris" and "Norris" and with maternal names "Mel", "Melinda", "Melissa" etc.

As best as I can tell, the closest the police ever came to finding Tegan was the discovery of a child named Teagan Collins (pseudonym), born on 14 September 1996. Her father's surname was Morris and her mother's surname was Collins (pseudonym). But enquiries revealed she was born at the Mater Hospital in Brisbane, Queensland. DNA testing revealed she was indeed the child of Ms Collins.

By 2008, no record had been found of Tegan having attended a doctor or having attended a school. Nor had any "Andrew Morris/Norris" been located.

In 2009, the Director of Public Prosecutions, Nicholas Cowdery QC, came to the view that there was sufficient evidence for Keli to be charged with murder. The charge was laid on 17 November 2009.

CHAPTER 2 - The Trial and Appeals

It is useful to set out the legal framework of Keli's trial and conviction.

The Trial – Judge and Jury

In New South Wales, most criminal trials are heard before a judge and a jury of 12 citizens. The jury is entrusted with deciding the facts of the case. It is sometimes called the "trier of fact". Jurors are required to swear an oath, or affirm, that they will deliver a true verdict according to the evidence. Generally, the jury's decision needs to be unanimous, although that requirement can be dispensed with in certain circumstances. The jury does not deliver reasons, although the reasoning can usually be inferred from the evidence and the way in which the trial was conducted.

The trial judge's primary function is to oversee the fairness of the trial. In particular, he/she has the final say over what material is admitted into evidence for the jury to consider. The trial judge also has the final say over how the jury is allowed to use the admitted evidence and what, if any, limitations should be placed upon it.

When all of the evidence has been tendered, and after both parties have presented their closing arguments about the evidence, the judge "instructs" or "directs" the jury as to how the law applies to the facts. The jury delivers its verdict. If the verdict is guilty, then the judge determines the penalty to be imposed upon the accused.

The trial of Keli (after preliminaries such as empanelment of the jury were completed) began on 9 August 2010. The Crown was represented by Senior Crown Prosecutor Mark Tedeschi QC and junior counsel, Huw Baker. I shall, in general, refer to Mr Tedeschi QC as "the Crown". Keli was represented by Keith Chapple SC and junior counsel Sylvie Sloane[23].

I turn now to consider some of the legal principles, concepts and issues that would inform the trial.

Elements of Offence and Standard of Proof

In order to prove the accused person is guilty of murder, the Crown must prove beyond reasonable doubt the following:

(a) that the victim is in fact <u>deceased</u>;
(b) that it was a <u>deliberate act</u> by the accused that caused the victim's death; and
(c) that the act causing the victim's death was done by the accused with the <u>intention</u> of killing the victim.

The onus of proving these three elements is upon the Crown.

If there is a plausible alternative hypothesis, consistent with innocence, that is capable of explaining the victim's death, then the Crown will have failed to discharge its onus of proof.

Generally speaking, the accused person never has to prove anything. The jury is generally not permitted to infer guilt against an accused because s/he does not offer evidence. The accused is said to have a right to silence. It is an important right. In this case, Keli exercised her right to silence. She elected to not give evidence.

Standard of Proof of Circumstances

Whilst each of the three core elements has to be proved beyond doubt, the Crown does not have to prove every single fact or circumstance beyond doubt. Generally speaking, a lesser standard of proof may

---

[23] The letters "QC" denote Mr Tedeschi's status as Queen's Counsel. The letters "SC" denote Mr Chapple's status as Senior Counsel. The senior status of each Counsel is the same. In New South Wales, in the early 1990's, the title was changed from "Queen's Counsel" to "Senior Counsel".

suffice for proof of each fact or circumstance. It depends upon the nature of the case:

> ". . . the [Crown] bears the onus of proving all the elements of the crime beyond reasonable doubt. That . . . does not mean that every fact – every piece of evidence – relied upon to prove an element by inference must itself be proved beyond reasonable doubt . . . [for example] the jury might quite properly draw [an inference of intent] having regard to the whole of the evidence, whether or not each individual piece of evidence relied upon is proved beyond reasonable doubt, provided they reach their <u>conclusion</u> [beyond reasonable doubt]. Indeed, the probative force of a mass of evidence may be cumulative, making it pointless to consider the degree of probability of each item of evidence separately"[24] [emphasis added]

Cases in which there are many circumstances, none of which individually are essential to the Crown's case, are often called "strands in a cable" cases. On the other hand, there will be cases in which one circumstance is indispensable to the Crown's case. The circumstance is said to be an indispensable link in the chain of proof. These are "link in the chain" cases. If the individual circumstance is that important, it may need to be proved beyond doubt[25].

Motive

The overarching motive alleged against Keli was that, for one reason or another, she wanted to avoid the responsibility of permanently caring for a child. This much was self-evident, having been spelled out by Keli herself in her police interviews. The Crown alleged further that there were several specific circumstances in Keli's case which heightened her desire to avoid permanent parenthood. One of these - the water polo

---

[24] *R v. Hillier* (2007) 233 ALR 634; 81 ALJR 886.[2007] HCA 13 per Dawson J at paragraph 6.

[25] *Shepherd v. R* (1990) 170 CLR 573, per McHugh J at page 593; [1990] HCA 56.

ambition - has already been touched upon. It was also alleged by the Crown that Keli had an active social life and sex life which she did not want interrupted by the need to care for a child. These matters will be dealt with in more detail at later points in this book. Suffice to say at this stage, motive is only a circumstance. It is not an essential element of the offence of murder. That being so, it is not, generally speaking, something that has to be proved:

> *"The law does not require impossibilities. The law recognises that the cause of the killing is sometimes so hidden in the mind and breast of the party who killed, that it cannot be fathomed, and as it does not require impossibilities, it does not require the jury to find it"* [sic][26]

The criminal law is generally concerned with the question of <u>whether</u> the accused person committed the crime, not <u>why</u>. Motive may be a clue to the question of whether the accused committed the crime, occasionally a significant one, but never more than a clue.

In the final analysis, motive tends to be important in close cases. The presence of motive is a circumstance that may help the Crown in a close contest. Absence of motive may help the defence in a close case. In a strong Crown case, motive is rarely decisive. Likewise, in a weak Crown case, motive cannot fill gaps, or act as a makeweight, for the Crown. In the result, motive is rarely a decisive, or turning, point in a criminal trial. I do not perceive Keli's case as one in which motive was decisive or was a turning point. My impression is that the Crown's case against Keli was otherwise a strong case. Motive was a welcome addition to the Crown's case, and it made Keli's conviction more likely[27], but it did not act as a makeweight.

---

[26] *Pointer v. United States* [1894] USSC 38; 151 US 396 at page 413.
[27] *The King v. Bell* [1911] AC 47, per Lord Atkinson at page 68.

Keli's Defence

In criminal cases, the accused's defence is not spelled out in a document. Therefore, the nature of the defence needs to be drawn out from the way in which the trial is conducted. My interpretation of the conduct of the trial by Keli's counsel is that her defence was to this effect:

1. the Crown's case is speculative and the evidence does not prove beyond doubt that Tegan is deceased or that Keli deliberately caused Tegan's death or that Keli intended to cause Tegan's death;
2. Keli does not deny she has told many lies, or half-truths, but she should not be convicted for murder just because she has told lies; and
3. Keli's account of giving Tegan to "Andrew Morris/Norris" is truthful.

Whilst ground number 3 was always inherently part of Keli's defence, the real thrust of it, as the trial developed, was that the Crown's case was speculative and murder could not be proved by merely proving Keli was a chronic liar.

A recurring strategy of the defence was to, in effect, seek to spin the Crown's case to make out Keli's defence. For example, the Crown tendered the evidence of Keli's other adoptions and terminations to prove Keli had a tendency to seek permanent solutions to her unwanted pregnancies. The defence relied on the same evidence to assert that the tendency disclosed was to seek lawful solutions to her problems. Thus, as the CCA would later state, it was not so much the facts that were in issue, but more the inferences to be drawn[28].

---

[28] *Lane v. R* [2013] NSWCCA 317, at paragraph 5.

Circumstantial Evidence

There are two types of evidence by which the Crown can seek to prove the elements of the offence – direct evidence and circumstantial evidence. Direct evidence is, for example, evidence from an eye-witness that s/he saw a crime being committed. Circumstantial evidence tends to be indirect, for example that the accused person had a motive for committing a crime. It then needs to be inferred from that fact (motive) that the accused person did commit the crime.

The Crown's case against Keli was based entirely upon circumstantial evidence. It is tempting to think that a case based on circumstantial evidence would be weaker than one based upon direct evidence. But this is not necessarily correct:

> " . . . *circumstantial evidence is very often the best. It is evidence of surrounding circumstances which, by undesigned coincidence, is capable of proving a proposition with the accuracy of mathematics. It is no derogation of evidence to say that it is circumstantial*"[29]

Mathematical accuracy might be overstating it, but there is no doubt that circumstantial evidence is often the strongest type of evidence:

> "*It is of the nature of many crimes that their perpetrators perform the deeds in secret. They do so in the hope of avoiding observation, detection and consequent prosecution and conviction. In such cases, a prosecutor must necessarily rely upon circumstantial evidence to prove the case against the accused. Circumstantial evidence 'can, and often does, clearly prove the commission of a criminal offence*'"[30]

---

[29] *Taylor, Weaver and Donovan* 21 Cr App R 20 at page 21, per Hewart LCJ.

[30] *De Gruchy v. R* [2002] 211 CLR 85, per Kirby J at paragraph 46, citing *Chamberlain v The Queen [No 2]* [1984] HCA 7; (1984) 153 CLR 521 at 599 per Brennan J.

and:

> *"Sometimes circumstantial evidence constituting a 'chain of other facts sworn to by many witnesses of undoubted credibility' can actually be stronger than disputable positive eye witness evidence"*[31]

In some cases, circumstances can give rise to strong inferences provided care is taken to avoid conjecture:

> *"Inference must be carefully distinguished from conjecture or speculation. There can be no inference unless there are objective facts from which to infer the other facts which it is sought to establish. In some cases the other facts can be inferred with as much practical certainty as if they had been actually observed. In other cases the inference does not go beyond reasonable probability. But if there are no positive proved facts from which the inference can be made, the method of inference fails and what is left is mere speculation or conjecture"*[32]

The jury must weigh all of the circumstances together and resist any temptation to deal with them in a piece-meal fashion:

> *"46. . . . It is of critical importance to recognise . . . all of the circumstances established by the evidence are to be considered and weighed in deciding whether there is an inference consistent with innocence reasonably open on the evidence.*
>
> . . .
>
> *49. . . . in a case depending on circumstantial evidence, the jury should not reject one circumstance because, considered alone, no inference of guilt can be drawn from it. It is well established*

---

[31] *De Gruchy v. R* [2002] 211 CLR 85, per Kirby J at paragraph 48, citing *Commonwealth v. Harman* 4 Pa St 269 at page 272.

[32] *Caswell v. Powell Duffryn Associated Collieries Ltd* [1940] AC 152.

that the jury must consider 'the weight which is to be given to the united force of all the circumstances put together': per Lord Cairns, in Belhaven and Stenton Peerage. . ."[33] [citation omitted]

Procedure – Joint Trials

The Crown sought to have the murder trial heard with, and at the same time as, the charges of false swearing of affidavits. To recap, Keli swore falsehoods in the affidavits relating to the adoptions of Trisha and Archie. Keli did not oppose the Crown's proposed course of having the false swearing and murder charges heard together. At first blush, this might have appeared a questionable course for Keli to adopt. To have murder and false swearing charges heard together creates the risk that the jurors will form an adverse view of the accused person as a result of the false swearing evidence and allow that to unduly influence their judgment on the murder charge. However, for reasons which will be developed, in my opinion, that risk was not realised in this case.

Evidence – The Lies

The use that the Crown could make of Keli's lies was one of the central issues of the trial and it was an ongoing issue. It was the subject of considerable attention on the part of Whealy J (even requiring appellate intervention at one point). The concern underlying all of this was, of course, that the jury might mistakenly find that because Keli was a liar, she must be a murderer. It is tempting to think that no rational juror would employ that type of reasoning, but the law is reluctant to make such an assumption. The law requires care to be taken to ensure that jurors do not misuse the evidence that is presented to them. Because this was an important feature of the trial, and because there appears to be misunderstanding and misinformation about the matter, it is appropriate to look closely at the lies and how they were dealt with at the trial.

---

[33] *R v. Hillier* [2007] HCA 13; (2007) 233 ALR 634; 81 ALJR 886 per Gummow, Hayne and Crennan JJ at paragraphs 46 to 49.

As we have seen, the Crown alleged that Keli had told some 95 lies about the pregnancies and related matters[34]. Some of these lies have already been highlighted. The lies were generally designed to prevent news of the pregnancies or births reaching Keli's family or friends. Three of the lies would be found by the jury to have been designed, in effect, to cover up murder and these will be considered later in some detail.

The evidence about the lies was mostly in written form, and contained in the business records of the following agencies:

1. Centacare
2. Anglicare
3. DOCS
4. Balmain Hospital
5. KGV Hospital
6. Ryde Hospital
7. Auburn Hospital
8. Police
9. Supreme Court

It is an oft-overlooked feature of this trial that the Crown's case was, in no small measure, based on documents, namely the business records of the above organisations. This lent strength to the Crown's case. One of Keli's major difficulties was that she was confronted with business records[35]. The practical significance was that it was difficult, if not impossible, for Keli to ever contest that she was something of a chronic liar. She became cornered into defending herself not on the basis that she was not a liar, but rather on the basis that she should not be convicted for murder for being a liar.

---

[34] This was a tally asserted by the Crown. Not having counted them myself, I will assume that the Crown's tally is correct and I think this is a safe course.

[35] Keli herself appears to have recognised this problem, writing to Ms Fung on 25 October 1999 that "*I can't lie anymore as the paperwork is there*".

Many of Keli's lies had a grain of truth. For example, in 1995 Keli told Balmain Hospital staff that she received care from a Dr Birkett in Perth. There was no Dr Birkett in Perth that had cared for her, but she did know a man by the name of Birkett who was a water polo player. The lies were built around these grains of truth.

It is useful to analyse just how, and on what basis, all of the lies came to be admitted into evidence.

The first time that attention was given to the lies was in the Crown's opening address to the jury (9 to 11 August 2010). Unsurprisingly, the Crown forcefully drew attention to Keli's lies.

Immediately after the Crown's opening, Whealy J gave, as a *"preparatory or introductory direction to the jury"* and a *"cautionary note on the topic"*, the following direction to the jury[36]:

> *"You must not fall into the error of thinking that if a person has told a lie then that lie in itself can prove guilt"*[37].

The topic of lies resurfaced on 23 August when the time came for evidence about the birth of Trisha to be adduced. Whealy J took this occasion to remind the jury of the *"preparatory"* direction he had earlier given[38]. There followed these comments which revealed how the topic was beginning to develop:

> *"11 . . . This is a trial in which the Crown will rely on a considerable number of lies. Some of these revolve around the birth of [Trisha], and perhaps the termination of pregnancies, at least one of them, and also there will be lies suggested surrounding the birth and adoption of [Archie]. These are essentially lies going to credibility and background in the murder charge.*

---

[36] *R v. Lane [No. 5]* [2010] NSWSC 1532, at paragraphs 11 and 20.

[37] *R v. Lane [No. 5]* [2010] NSWSC 1532, at paragraph 20.

[38] *R v. Lane [No. 5]* [2010] NSWSC 1532, at paragraph 15.

12. Importantly for the Crown case in the way it wishes to lead matters to the jury, there will be a need to consider whether any lies told in connection with the birth of Tegan and, critically, what happened to Tegan after her birth may be relied upon by the Crown as evidence of consciousness of guilt.

15. . . . the evidence relating to this category of lies has not yet emerged" [39]

Thus, it was emerging that the lies would fall into different categories and be tendered by the Crown for different purposes (i.e. to prove different matters).

By early October, most of Keli's 95 lies had been admitted into evidence, albeit only as contextual or background evidence at that stage. Once admitted, the lies became relevant to assessment of Keli's credibility. That is, the jury could use them as evidence diminishing the credibility of Keli's account of giving Tegan to "Andrew Norris". But the jury could not take the lies as (direct) proof that Keli murdered Tegan.

On 6 October, the Crown applied to have certain evidence about the lies used in an additional way, which was to prove that Keli had a tendency to do or say certain things, namely:

(i)   adopt solutions in relation to the three live births (Trisha in 1995, Tegan in 1996 and Archie in 1999) which resulted in her being permanently rid of responsibility for the care of each child;

(ii) fabricate matters relating to the paternity of the three babies so as to prevent any contact with, or by, the real fathers and keep the pregnancies secret from family and friends; and

(iii) invent fictitious identities ("Aaron Williams" and "Andrew Morris/Norris") as the fathers of the babies;[40]

---

[39] *R v. Lane [No. 5]* [2010] NSWSC 1532, at paragraphs 11, 12 and 15.

[40] The precise evidence which was the subject of the application was set out in notices under section 101 of the *Evidence Act 1995* (NSW). I have not seen those notices.

The Crown's application to have the lies tendered for these purposes was opposed by Keli. After hearing argument from the Crown and the defence, Whealy J determined that the Crown could use the lies for the purpose of seeking to prove that Keli had a tendency to do and say the things set out. Thus, by this stage of the trial, the lies were in evidence as background, credibility and tendency evidence in the murder charge, although none of this meant that it was open to the jury to reason directly that Keli murdered Tegan[41].

On 3 November 2010, the Crown applied to have a select group of three of Keli's lies admitted into evidence for yet another purpose which was to prove that Keli had a consciousness, or awareness, of guilt[42]. The three lies in question were:

1. The Perth Couple Lie
   Keli stated in the fax to Ms Fung (25 October 1999) that Tegan *"lived with a family in Perth"*.
2. The Andrew Morris Lie
   Keli told Kehoe that she handed Tegan over to Andrew Morris.
3. The Andrew Norris Lie
   Keli told Gaut that she handed Tegan over to Andrew Norris.

This was an important moment in the trial and conviction of Keli. The Crown was now asking that the jury be permitted to treat these three lies as going beyond evidence merely diminishing the credibility of Keli's story and beyond proving Keli had a tendency to do and say certain things. The Crown was now seeking to enable the jury to use these three (alleged) lies as evidence from which it could reason directly that Keli murdered Tegan. The High Court's judgment

---

[41] The lies were also tendered for the purpose of proving motive. It is unnecessary to consider this for present purposes.

[42] The Crown also sought to have certain conduct admitted as evidence of consciousness of guilt, for example Keli's avoidance of Detective Gaut's phone calls. Ultimately, the Crown was prohibited from using this conduct as evidence of consciousness of guilt and I will omit consideration of this matter.

in *Edwards v. The Queen* (1993) 178 CLR 193 was the seminal Australian judgment on the admissibility of lies as consciousness of guilt. The following passage from the joint judgment of Deane, Dawson and Gaudron JJ is instructive:

> "... *not every lie told by an accused provides evidence probative of guilt. It is only if the accused is telling a lie because he perceives the truth is inconsistent with his innocence that the telling of the lie may constitute evidence [from which the jury can directly reason guilt]. In other words,* <u>*in telling the lie the accused must be acting as if he were guilty. It must be a lie which an innocent person would not tell.*</u> *That is why the lie must be deliberate. Telling an untruth inadvertently cannot be indicative of guilt. And the lie must relate to a material issue because the telling of it must be explicable only on the basis that the truth would implicate the accused in the offence with which he is charged. It must be for that reason that he tells the lie. To say that the lie must spring from a realisation or consciousness of guilt is really another way of saying the same thing. It is to say that the accused must be lying because he is conscious that 'if he tells the truth, the truth will convict him'"*[43] [emphasis added]

The Crown's proposed use of these lies as evidence of consciousness of guilt was opposed by Keli. After hearing argument from the Crown and the defence, in a judgment delivered on 3 November, Whealy J ruled in Keli's favour and refused to allow the Crown to rely on the three lies as evidence of consciousness of guilt[44]. However, on 16 November, after hearing argument, the New South Wales Court of Criminal Appeal (hereafter "CCA") overruled Whealy J[45]. The CCA was constituted by three justices and the decision was unanimous.

---

[43] *Edwards v. The Queen* (1993) 178 CLR 193; [1993] HCA 63.

[44] *R v. Lane [No.13]* [2010] NSWSC 1540.

[45] *R v. Lane* [2011] NSWCCA 157. Stephen Odgers SC and Ms Sloane represented Keli on this occasion. Mr Tedeschi QC and Mr Baker continued to represent the Crown.

Therefore, the Crown was permitted to tender the lies as evidence of consciousness, or awareness, of guilt. If the jury accepted that Keli's statements were deliberate lies, and that these lies were told out of consciousness of guilt, then it was permitted to reason directly from them that Keli murdered Tegan. In other words, in telling these lies Keli was acting as if she was guilty of murder (or was telling the sorts of lies that an innocent person would not tell). It follows, in my opinion, that it was fair to characterise these lies as lies told with a view to covering up murder. The Crown had already been in a powerful position (the credibility of Keli's story was considerably diminished by this stage), but it seems to me the admission of the three lies as evidence of awareness of guilt put the Crown in a virtually impregnable position.

Jury Verdict and Judge's Sentence

On 13 December 2010, the jury delivered a majority guilty verdict on the murder charge. Eleven jurors had favoured conviction and one had favoured acquittal. Unanimous guilty verdicts were delivered on the false swearing charges.

On 15 April 2011, Whealy J sentenced Keli to 18 years of imprisonment commencing 13 December 2010. A non-parole period of 13 years 5 months was imposed, meaning Keli would become eligible for parole on 12 May 2024. Keli was sentenced to terms of imprisonment of nine months, nine months and twelve months respectively for the three offences of false swearing of affidavits. These sentences were to be served concurrently with the sentence for murder.

Sentencing requires an assessment of, amongst other things, the nature of the offence. The less heinous the offence, the less the sentence. The less premeditation, the less the sentence. Whealy J determined, essentially, that the premeditation was only of a short duration and arose out of Keli's despair at the circumstances in which she found herself. This was about the most favourable finding that Keli could expect. Whealy J thought it was a *"relatively, although not completely, spontaneous act*" committed in desperate circumstances[46]. He appeared to accept the evidence of Dr Michael Diamond, psychiatrist, to the effect that Keli had a disordered personality:

> ". . . *[Keli's] decision to bring her daughter's life to an end was made in a situation of some desperation and was contributed to, in part, by the dysfunctional complexities arising from aspects of her disordered personality*"[47]

This will receive further attention in a later chapter.

Appeal to the New South Wales Court of Criminal Appeal

On 23 July 2013, Keli appealed to the CCA against her conviction. (She did not appeal against her sentence.) The Crown was represented by Jennie Girdham SC and Huw Baker. Keli was represented by Winston Terracini SC and James Trevallion.

Appeals against conviction are normally heard by three justices[48]. Justices of appeal are the most senior jurists in New South Wales. They are the justices with responsibility for assessing the fairness of first instance trials. The CCA is a supervisory jurisdiction – it supervises criminal trials. It is the highest criminal court in New South Wales.

Section 6 of the *Criminal Appeal Act 1912* (NSW) prescribes that the appellant (Keli) must establish one of three circumstances in order to succeed in an appeal:

(i)   the verdict was unreasonable or cannot be supported by the evidence;

(ii) there was a wrong decision on a question of law; or

(iii) there was, for any other reason, a miscarriage of justice.

---

[46] *R v. Lane* [2011] NSWSC 289, at paragraph 43.

[47] *R v. Lane* [2011] NSWSC 289, at paragraph 44.

[48] A panel of five judges can be constituted in cases involving matters of significant legal principle. Keli's case was not such a case.

The CCA must undertake its own independent examination of the evidence to determine whether it was open to the jury to convict the appellant[49]. The appeal is akin to, but not the same as, a re-hearing of the trial. By its nature, it is a rigorous and exhaustive examination of the fairness of the trial.

An appeal is a hard road to travel. The jury's decision deserves respect and some degree of deference because the jury had the advantage of seeing and hearing the witnesses and the general unfolding of the evidence. It is not enough that an error was made at the trial. The appellant must establish that the error was productive of a miscarriage of justice.

The grounds of Keli's appeal were as follows[50]:

1. Whealy J erred in failing to allow the jury to consider an alternative charge of manslaughter.
2. The trial miscarried because of the content of the Crown's closing address, in particular he expressed personal opinions and he insinuated that Keli was a person of bad character in that she would mistreat or malign innocent people.
3. The trial miscarried because the Crown proposed to the jury that they keep in mind a series of (rhetorical) questions when they listen to the defence counsel's closing submission, which had the effect of reversing the onus of proof.
4. The defence counsel (Chapple SC) should have applied to have the false swearing charges separated from the murder charges.
5. Whealy J should have directed the jury that the charge of infanticide was an alternative.
6. Whealy J should have discharged the jury after the Crown speculated to the jury about the whereabouts of Tegan's body.

---

[49] *M v. The Queen* (1994) 181 CLR 487.
[50] I have modified the numeration for the purposes of this book.

7. Whealy J erred in allowing the Crown to cross-examine the witness Peter Clark.
8. The verdict was unreasonable and could not be supported by the evidence.
9. The trial miscarried because the defence counsel (Chapple SC) failed to ask Whealy J to direct the jury that Keli was prejudiced by the delay in the prosecution.

Keli only needed to succeed on one of these grounds in order to have her conviction overturned. She did not need to succeed on all of the grounds.

Ground 5 was abandoned by Keli during the hearing of the appeal. Most of the other grounds of appeal are covered elsewhere in this book. I shall only deal with grounds 1, 2, 3 and 9 at this juncture.

Ground 1 – Alternative Count of Manslaughter

This ground of appeal received long and detailed consideration in the CCA. I think it can be fairly said to boil down to this. A finding of manslaughter requires evidence about the manner and cause of death. In other words, it requires an explanation about how and why the death occurred. For example, a finding of manslaughter by criminal negligence requires evidence that establishes a duty of care was owed by the accused person, and that the duty was breached and that the breach caused the death – all matters that require evidence about the manner and cause of death. In this case, there was no evidence of the manner and cause of death. Therefore, it was impossible for the jury to find, for example, manslaughter by criminal negligence. The jury could only reason that if they were satisfied that Tegan's death came about unlawfully, then it had to be murder. In the CCA's words: *"the evidence was capable of establishing that [Keli] intended to kill Tegan, and was not such as to establish any other, or lesser, intention"*[51].

---

[51] *R v. Lane* [2013] NSWCCA 317 at paragraph 287.

Put simply, there was evidence of intent, but there was no evidence of accident. It was an "all or nothing" case.

Ground 2 – The Crown's Personal Opinions and Insinuations

Keli argued that the Crown improperly expressed his personal opinions when he uttered to the jury the words "*come on*" when addressing the topic of Keli having filled in the Medicare registration form in respect of Tegan and in particular Keli's explanation that this had been done in case Tegan had ever been returned to her care. The argument was, basically, that the Crown was scoffing at Keli's explanation.

In dealing with Keli's complaint, the CCA noted that the use of rhetoric, less formal language or vernacular phrases was not inconsistent with the duties of a prosecutor. The CCA rejected the contention that the Crown had overstepped the mark[52].

Keli also complained that the Crown had insinuated in his closing address to the jury that Keli was a person of bad character. The gist of this complaint was that the Crown had insinuated that Keli had exploited Ms Fung to her own advantage and, as I understand it, that Keli had potentially misled her children, Trisha and Archie, in respect of the true identities of their fathers.

The CCA considered that, in the context of the obvious credibility issues at the trial, the Crown's comments were not gratuitous or inappropriate[53]. The CCA commented that this may explain why defence counsel had not objected to them at the trial, which of itself may have been another reason for rejection of Keli's appeal complaint.

Ground 3 – The Crown's Questions

Keli's next complaint was about a series of questions posed in a rhetorical fashion by the Crown in his closing address to the jury at the trial. Keli's argument was that these questions had the effect of

---

[52] *R v. Lane* [2013] NSWCCA 317 at paragraph 117.
[53] *R v. Lane* [2013] NSWCCA 317 at paragraph 120.

reversing the onus of proof and misleading the jury into thinking that Keli was guilty unless she actually supplied the answers.

The CCA considered that disparaging the defence case by posing rhetorical questions in this manner did create a risk of reversal of the onus of proof. However, the court also pointed out that Keli's counsel did not complain about the Crown's questions. And Whealy J gave a comprehensive warning to the jury that Keli had no onus to supply answers. Whealy J also spoke to the jury of the danger of reversing the onus of proof. The CCA ultimately considered that if the Crown's questions had any deleterious effect, it was no more than transitory. The ground of appeal failed[54].

Ground 9 – Delay in Prosecution

In this ground of appeal, Keli contended that the delay between the time of the offence and the trial prejudiced her ability to have a fair defence[55].

It is not unusual for counsel to assert at trial that delay has caused the defence to be unable to properly investigate and test the Crown's case. At the trial, it was open to Keli to ask Whealy J to direct the jury about this potential unfairness. However, Keli did not seek such a direction. In dealing with this appeal point, the CCA considered it could be safely assumed that there was a strategic reason for Keli declining to ask for such a direction at the trial. The problem for Keli would have been that such a direction would have necessitated an examination of the reasons for the delay. This would inevitably draw attention to the significant role that Keli's lies played in thwarting and delaying the investigation. It was not in Keli's interests to draw attention to her lies. Therefore, being satisfied that there was likely a tactical reason for Keli not seeking the direction at the trial, the CCA rejected the ground of appeal[56].

There were other conceivable reasons for rejecting this ground of appeal but it is unnecessary to consider them.

---

[54] *Lane v. R* [2013] NSWCCA 317 at paragraph 132.
[55] *Longman v. The Queen* [1989] HCA 60; 168 CLR 79.
[56] *Lane v. R* [2013] NSWCCA 317 at paragraph 174.

The CCA's Reasoning and Determination

On 13 December 2013, exactly three years after the jury had convicted Keli, the CCA, comprising Chief Justice Tom Bathurst and Justices Carolyn Simpson and Christine Adamson, unanimously rejected all of Keli's grounds of appeal and dismissed the appeal[57].

Reference has previously been made to the three core elements of the offence of murder, each of which has to be proved beyond reasonable doubt by the Crown : (1) that the victim is in fact <u>deceased</u> (2) that it was a <u>deliberate</u> act of the accused that caused the death and (3) that the accused <u>intended</u> to kill the victim.

As to the first element (death), the CCA observed that, given the way the trial had been conducted, there were only really two alternatives open to the jury: either Tegan was dead or she had been given to her natural father[58]. The CCA considered the evidence *"convincingly excluded any reasonable possibility of the second alternative"*[59]. The CCA considered it significant that Keli had denied having a child in 1996 when speaking to Mr Borovnik and had repeated that denial to Ms Fung. Significance was also attached to the following matters:

- Keli's notification to the RDMP that she would not require their services and that a homebirth midwife would be taking over Tegan's care (no mention of "Andrew Morris/Norris");
- Keli's attempt to assimilate the "Perth couple" with "Andrew Morris/Norris" and "Mel" in the interview with Gaut; and
- the police investigation having *"virtually excluded any possibility that there existed a man named Andrew Morris/ Andrew Norris"*[60].

As to the second element of the offence (deliberate act), the CCA's reasoning was succinct:

---

[57] *Lane v. R* [2013] NSWCCA 317.

[58] *Lane v. R* [2013] NSWCCA 317 at paragraph 278.

[59] *Lane v. R* [2013] NSWCCA 317 at paragraph 281.

[60] *Lane v. R* [2013] NSWCCA 317 at paragraphs 279 and 281.

"Once it is concluded that the child is dead, it is a short step, and an inevitable one, to the further conclusion that it was the act of [Keli] that caused the death . . . the evidence established beyond reasonable doubt that it was an act of [Keli] that caused Tegan's death"[61]

The CCA observed that *"[o]f course, the mere fact that [Keli] told untruths about the disposal of the child does not, of itself, establish that [Keli] killed the child. It is, however, one powerful item of evidence in a circumstantial case"*[62].

As to the third element (intent), the CCA reiterated its conclusion on the question of manslaughter. That is to say, that given there was evidence capable of supporting intentional death but not capable of supporting a finding of some sort of accidental death, a finding of intent was inevitable.

The CCA's judgment was unanimous. The language of the judgment was emphatic. It remains the most authoritative, detailed and impartial statement about Keli's trial, and the events generally, that exists. It is, by its nature, definitive of whether Keli got a fair trial. But *Exposed* relegated the appeal to a single note at the end of the documentary. When I engaged with social media about the documentary, and the case generally, it became evident that hardly anybody had read the CCA judgment or had any idea of its significance. The perception seemed to be that the CCA provided a perfunctory rubber-stamp endorsement of the jury's verdict. Nothing could be further from the truth.

Application for Special Leave to Appeal to High Court of Australia

On 15 August 2014, Keli sought special leave to appeal to the High Court of Australia ("HCA"). This was not an appeal, as such. It was an application for leave (permission) to appeal from the CCA's decision. The Crown was again represented by Jennie Girdham SC and Huw

---

[61] *Lane v. R* [2013] NSWCCA 317 at paragraph 284.
[62] *Lane v. R* [2013] NSWCCA 317 at paragraph 280.

Baker. Keli was represented by Winston Terracini SC, James Trevallion and Elizabeth Nicholson.

Special leave to appeal to the HCA is difficult to obtain. Section 35 of the *Judiciary Act 1903* (Cth.) requires that the appeal be related to a question of law "*that is of public importance, whether because of its general application or otherwise*". The application for special leave was heard by two justices of the HCA, Justices Bell and Keane. After hearing submissions from Keli's counsel, the Crown was told by the Court that it would not be called upon to make submissions. The Court's judgment was "*that the decision of the [CCA] is not attended with sufficient doubt to warrant the grant of leave. Special leave to appeal is refused*"[63].

There are no further avenues of appeal for Keli. There is, however, one more legal mechanism available to Keli, namely a review of her conviction pursuant to the *Crimes (Appeal and Review) Act 2001* (NSW). It is understood that an application for such a review has been made. Although I have not seen the application, it can be safely assumed it is based upon the matters that were the subject of the *Exposed* documentary which are considered in the following chapter of this book. As at the time of writing, the outcome of the application for review is not known.

---

[63] *Lane v. The Queen* [2014] HCATrans 171.

CHAPTER 3 - The ABC documentary : *Exposed*

In late 2018, the ABC broadcasted *Exposed.* It comprised three episodes. *Exposed* presented various claims about the trial and conviction of Keli[64].

Exposed's promotional publicity implied that it would make revelations about Keli's conviction. Viewers were told there's always a *"story behind the story".* However, many of the claims resembled arguments pressed by Keli at her trial or complaints made by Keli at the hearing of her appeal, or arguments disavowed by Keli herself. *Exposed* appears to have been an attempt to re-agitate Keli's court losses. This time the chosen forum was the proverbial court of public opinion.

I will deal with the various *Exposed* claims but not in any particular order, much less in the order in which they appeared in *Exposed.* I have sought to paraphrase the claims. I apologise in advance if I have unfairly characterised any of the material that was aired.

Claim 1 – Keli's senior counsel, Mr Chapple SC, was only briefed three weeks before the trial started, the inference being that he was unable to properly prepare for the trial and accordingly Keli was unfairly prejudiced[65]

---

[64] I am using the term "claim" in a generic sense. Some of the claims were veiled. They might equally be called insinuations or suggestions, depending on the way each was presented. Some arose in a passing sort of way making it hard to judge just how seriously they were being pressed. But they all manifested considerable inaccuracy.

[65] *Exposed,* Episode 3, at 0.23.

A barrister, Peter Hamill SC, who represented Keli at the inquest in 2005, was interviewed by *Exposed* and asked about the late briefing of defence counsel (Mr Chapple SC). Mr Hamill asserted on camera that three weeks did not sound like enough time to prepare for the trial, the impression being created that three weeks was in fact not enough time. However, in my view, the best judge of whether Mr Chapple had enough time to prepare was Mr Chapple himself. I have not seen any evidence of complaint by Mr Chapple that he was prejudiced by having insufficient time to prepare for the trial. Moreover, in the CCA, there was no complaint from Keli or her new lawyers (Terracini SC and Trevallion) that Mr Chapple had been forced on to trial in a way which prejudiced Keli.

It has been suggested Keli may have been to blame for the "late" briefing of Mr Chapple because she had been holding out while trying to get somebody else[66]. This is a common enough scenario, but I have not been able to verify it in Keli's case. On 24 May 2010, some 10 weeks before the due date for the trial (9 August), Keli's junior counsel, Ms Sloane, told the Supreme Court duty judge, Justice Megan Latham, that it had been ascertained that eight senior counsel were available to represent Keli at the trial. *Exposed's* viewers were not told about this. Why it took a further seven weeks to brief Mr Chapple remains unexplained.

Furthermore, there are reasonably strict rules in New South Wales about when and in what circumstances barristers must accept, or may refuse, briefs[67]. In particular, barristers are subject to the so-called "cab-rank" rule which provides that a barrister must accept a brief if, relevantly, the brief is within his *"capacity, skill and experience"*[68]. It follows that, if Mr Chapple considered the brief delivered to him three weeks before the trial was not within his *"capacity, skill and experience"*, he was entitled to refuse it. That he did not refuse it gives rise to an

---

[66] Chin R., *Nice Girl,* Simon & Schuster, 2011, page 267. .

[67] *Legal Profession Uniform Conduct (Barristers) Rules 2014,* known in 2010 as the New South Wales Bar Rules. I shall refer to them as "the Bar Rules".

[68] Rule 17 of the Bar Rules.

inference that he considered it was within his *"capacity, skill and experience"* notwithstanding the time allowed for preparation.

Finally, Rule 111 of the Bar Rules provides, relevantly, as follows:

> *111.   A barrister must promptly inform the instructing solicitor or the client as soon as the barrister has reasonable grounds to believe that there is a real possibility that the barrister will be unable to . . . do the work required by the brief in the time stipulated . . ."*

There is no evidence of which I am aware of Mr Chapple SC informing his solicitor or Keli of a real possibility he would be unable to prepare for the trial in the available three weeks. The irresistible inference is that he did not consider there was such a possibility. That is to say, he considered he was able to prepare.

Finally, my research has led me to conclude that Mr Chapple SC conducted Keli's defence competently. This is not conclusive of whether he had adequate time to prepare, but it suggests that he did. It also suggests that his performance, and the result, would have been no different had he had more time to prepare.

In conclusion, it was unlikely that Keli was significantly, or at all, prejudiced by Mr Chapple SC being briefed three weeks before the trial started.

Claim 2 – One of the motives alleged by the Crown – that Keli did not want her prospects of representing Australia in water polo at the 2000 Olympics compromised by having responsibility for a baby – was false. Keli was never realistically a candidate for selection for the Australian water polo team for the 2000 Olympic Games.

Exposed broadcasted an interview with a water polo coach who stated that, in effect, Keli was not a candidate for national selection for the Olympics. However, the interview begged a number of questions, not least of which was whether Keli's allegedly poor selection prospects were communicated to her. It appears not. In late 1997, Keli asked ACPE if she could take time out from studies to concentrate on making the Australian team[69]. In February 1998, Keli again wrote to ACPE asking for deferral of her practical teaching at least partly on account of her ongoing ambition to make the 2000 national team for the Olympics. Thus, whatever the coach(es) may have thought, Keli appears to have remained determined to make the national team. She was either not told she was not a selection prospect or she was oblivious to what was said to her.

It is worth having a closer look at Keli's fledgling water polo career and in particular at the timing of some of her achievements.

As we have seen, Keli represented New South Wales at an under-21's tournament in Perth in January 1995. In March 1995, Keli told social workers that she did not want her ambition to represent Australia hindered. In July 1995, she was selected to represent Australia in an under-20's international tournament in Canada. In 1997, she represented New South Wales at senior level. These appear to have been high achievements and, on the face of it, stepping stones to selection as a national senior player. On any view of it, at least in the period 1995 to 1997, Keli seems to have been an elite player. She seems to have had good reason to consider herself a contender for future international selection.

It appears that, objectively, her chances of making the national team may have started to peter out after, say, 1997. The representative honours appear to have plateaued, or even declined, from 1998 onwards. But she seems to have been a genuine selection prospect in 1995 to 1997. It looks as though she was being groomed for senior national selection during those years. Even if her selection prospects dwindled after 1997, that was irrelevant to Keli's motivation to kill Tegan in 1996. *Exposed* mentioned nothing of Keli's statements to the social workers, nor the communications to ACPE, nor the precise extent and timing of her water polo achievements by 1997.

---

[69] Chin, *Nice Girl*, p. 88.

Moreover, the Crown's case on motive was not as narrow as simply alleging that water polo was the motive. The Crown alleged several motives. The Crown's case was, in its broadest sense, that Keli would not take on the permanent responsibility of a baby. Indeed, Keli herself largely made out the Crown's case on motive when she told Kehoe in 2001 that she was unable to look after a baby.

In any event, it was unnecessary for the Crown to prove motive[70]. That the Crown did prove motive was a welcome addition to its case, but its absence would have been unlikely to result in a different outcome in the circumstances of this case. The evidence in favour of guilt was otherwise ample. It was not a borderline case.

The CCA would later sum up the issue of motive in this way:

> *"We do not accept the proposition that the evidence said to establish motive was weak. There was strong evidence that [Keli] did not wish to accept responsibility for a child. In any event, it is not essential that the Crown establish a motive; evidence tending to establish a motive was, in this case, one of many elements making up a circumstantial case. It was not necessary that it be proved beyond reasonable doubt. Even if it were correct to characterise that evidence as weak, that does not diminish the strength of the numerous other items of evidence in the Crown case that were not explained"[71]*

In conclusion, the water polo motive alleged by the Crown was not false. Even if Keli was not considered by others as a candidate for national selection, that was not, at least in 1996, something that ameliorated her own intense desire to progress to national selection.

Claim 3 – There was no evidence, or insufficient evidence, that Keli murdered Tegan[72]

---

[70] *Pointer v. United States* [1894] USSC 38; 151 US 396 at p.143; *De Gruchy v. R* (2002) 211 CLR 85.

[71] *Lane v. R* [2013] NSWCCA 317, at paragraph 276.

[72] *Exposed*, Episode 1 at 0.06, Episode 3, at 0.18.

This claim was erroneous. There was abundant evidence of murder. The CCA would later describe the guilty verdict as "*amply open to the jury*"[73]. The CCA also referred to the "*great deal*" of evidence that Tegan was deceased and that her death was caused by Keli[74].

A Dr Michelle Ruyters, from the Bridge of Hope Innocence Initiative, was interviewed on *Exposed* and stated:

> "*There's no evidence of a death, no evidence of a body, no evidence of a homicide, there's no witnesses, there's no confession*"[75]

This statement was riddled with error.

As to the issue of death, as the CCA stated, there was a "*great deal*" of evidence. There was evidence that many of the normal markers of live human existence in Australia, such as birth registration, could not be found. There was evidence that Tegan had never attended a doctor. There was evidence she had never attended a school. There was evidence that the police had been unable to find any trace of Tegan despite going to enormous lengths to find her. There was also the evidence (previously discussed) to which the CCA attached significance (lack of mention of "Andrew" to Mr Borovnik and others, and so on). The evidence may have been circumstantial, but it was nonetheless powerful.

There was ample evidence of homicide. There was evidence that Keli sought to cover up the murder. There was evidence that Keli was the last person verified as being with Tegan alive. There was evidence that Keli's explanation of Tegan's whereabouts was devoid of credibility. There was also evidence that Keli had motive(s) to murder Tegan. And so on.

As to witnesses, some 80 witnesses testified, consuming four months of trial time, longer than some Royal Commissions. Witnesses testified about all manner of things, for example, the lack of visitors during Keli's stay at Auburn Hospital, the time of her departure from

---

[73] *Lane v. R* [2013] NSWCCA 317, at paragraph 291.

[74] *Lane v. R* [2013] NSWCCA 317, at paragraph 20.

[75] *Exposed*, Episode 3, at 0.18.

the Hospital, her demeanour at the wedding and the police searches for "Andrew"/Tegan. These witnesses didn't see the murder but their evidence was important. And Keli was confronted with something just as compelling as witnesses – incontrovertible business records.

It was true there was no confession. But the absence of a confession is not probative of guilt or innocence. And there were numerous admissions by Keli, for example her statement to Kehoe that she was not able to care for a baby and her statement to Ms Fung that she had lied. And several more admissions were made by Keli when interviewed by *Exposed*. For example, she admitted the high degree of trauma associated with the terminations and first adoption (consistent with the Crown's case). She also admitted her uncertainty about the surname of "Andrew".

It was true there was no body. But this does not preclude guilt for murder. The absence of a body may make investigation and prosecution harder, but if the other evidence of guilt is strong enough it will not preclude guilt. If the absence of a body precluded guilt, then the question of guilt or innocence would tend to depend upon how effectively the accused person disposed of the body. Self-evidently, this would be absurd.

Exposed also referred viewers to an *"internal brief questioning whether the circumstantial evidence was enough to charge Keli Lane with murder"*[76]. Sharon Rhodes, who was a police officer involved in the investigation of the case, was interviewed. The *"internal brief"* document was shown to Ms Rhodes. Ms Rhodes spoke these words as she appeared to read from the document:

> *"the evidence does not establish a motive beyond reasonable doubt"*

Without disrespect to Ms Rhodes, the value of this statement was questionable given that the Crown did not have to establish motive (beyond reasonable doubt, or at all).

There was then this exchange between Ms Rhodes and the reporter:

---

[76] *Exposed*, Episode 3, at 0.10.

Rhodes: *By November 2008 to be completely honest, we had not reached the standard of beyond reasonable doubt, so we weren't in a position to charge Keli Lane at that point so we sought legal advice*

Q.:   *. . . it hadn't . . . met the bar for murder?*

Rhodes: *It hadn't met the standard of proof required*

Q.:   *After, gosh, two years investigation in homicide, several years with Manly, a Coronial inquest?*

Rhodes: *It still wasn't there. So we wanted, I wanted, to know whether or not it would ever get there, or we were wasting our time and should we, um, stop, and that was why we sent it to the [Director of Public Prosecutions] for a legal advising*[77]

A powerful impression was created by these exchanges, assisted by the deeply grave tone of the reporter's voice, that the Crown's evidence was insufficient to prove murder. However, the "*internal brief*" appeared to be dated 2008. Everything said was apparently referable to the state of the evidence in 2008. This had no relevance by the time of the trial in 2010. By 2010, the evidence was plainly sufficient, given that the jury convicted Keli, and the conviction was confirmed by unanimous decision of the CCA. Why *Exposed* saw fit to highlight the state of the evidence in 2008 is quite beyond me.

Claim 4 – The Crown prosecutor unfairly prejudiced Keli's defence by suggesting in his opening that Keli may have disposed of Tegan's body at the Sydney Olympic site at Homebush[78]

It was true that the Crown introduced into his opening speech to the jury a comment to the effect that Tegan may have been dumped at the Olympic site. He did so in the absence of evidence to that effect. This was impermissible because it created the risk that the jury would take

---

[77] *Exposed*, Episode 3, at 0.10.

[78] *Exposed*, Episode 3, at 0.26.

into account something about which there was no evidence. Left at that, it was capable of causing unfair prejudice to Keli. However, it was not left at that. It was cured. The next day the Crown withdrew his comment to the jury.

Keli would later complain to the CCA that the Crown's withdrawal of the comment was insufficient to cure the problem and that the jury ought to have been discharged. The CCA considered Keli's complaint and then rejected it. The CCA observed, in its unanimous judgment, that Keli's trial counsel (Mr Chapple SC) did not seek to have the jury discharged. He appeared to have elected to take forensic advantage of the Crown's error to highlight Keli's own argument that the Crown's case was speculative. That is, he elected to try to turn the Crown's comment around to Keli's strategic advantage. That being so, "*no unfairness attended the process*"[79]. The CCA stated that that was sufficient to dispose of Keli's complaint. That may be so. But it does not mean there were not other reasons for rejection of Keli's complaint. One that springs to mind is that the jury was fresh from having sworn its oath to decide the matter solely by reference to the evidence. Having heard the Crown state pointedly that the Homebush disposal was not part of the evidence, it was unlikely they would take it into account in direct avoidance of their recently sworn oath.

Exposed did not tell viewers about the CCA's determination. When that, together with the Crown's withdrawal of the offending comment, is taken into account, it is abundantly clear in my opinion that the Crown's comment about the disposal of Tegan's body was of no consequence.

Claim 5 – Whealy J considers he might have had a doubt if he was the trier of fact, and he had never been certain about Keli's guilt[80]

It is trite that Whealy J was not the trier of fact. Therefore, his opinion about what he might have thought, had he been the trier

---

[79] *Lane v. R* [2013] NSWCCA 317 at paragraph 142.

[80] By the time of *Exposed*, Whealy J had retired from the judiciary. However, I will continue to refer to him as "Whealy J".

of fact, was irrelevant. It was equally trite that the language of his comment was not particularly convincing or probative of whether Keli was guilty or innocent.

Moreover, viewers were not told whether Whealy J was made aware by *Exposed* that since the trial Keli had (a) yet again changed her story about the hand-over of Tegan (b) yet again modified her story about the surname of Tegan's biological father and (c) confirmed the Crown's case advanced at the trial about the trauma associated with the terminations and first adoption. It is hard to accept that Whealy J might have a doubt about Keli's guilt if he was aware of this material.

To digress briefly, in my opinion Whealy J's television appearance was undesirable because it was capable of creating the perception of a disagreement between judge and jury as to the appropriate verdict. That undesirable state of affairs has now become something of a reality. To my observation, Keli's supporters rely upon Whealy J's comments and tend to embellish them into statements positively supportive of Keli's innocence. They go on to contend that Whealy J was right and the jury was wrong, and the system (including the jury's verdict) is rotten. Even as this book nears publication, almost 12 months after *Exposed* went to air, I find myself repeatedly engaged in discussions on social media with persons in Australia and from overseas about the perceived conflict between judge and jury in this case. With respect to Whealy J, he should have known there was a good chance his comments would be taken this way.

The potential for strife brought about by the perception of inconsistent verdicts has long been recognised by the law[81]. Confidence in the rule of law can only be eroded where that perception arises, particularly where the inconsistency is between judge and jury in the same case. In my respectful opinion, Whealy J's interaction with the media had the potential to bring the law into disrepute.

---

[81] For example, various established principles exist to ensure that different court proceedings that arise out of the same factual scenario should normally be tried together: *Ross v. R* [2012] NSWCCA 207; *R v. Demirok* [1976] VR 244 at page 254; *Demirok v. R* (1977) 137 CLR 20; *R v. Fernando* [1999] NSWCCA 66.

Furthermore, conspicuous by its absence from *Exposed* was any questioning of Whealy J about whether or not he considered Keli received a fair trial. Ensuring a fair trial was his responsibility as the trial judge and he would be well placed to comment. It seems inconceivable that Whealy J would consider the trial was not fair. It can surely be safely assumed, although he was not asked about it, that Whealy J would think, and say, that Keli in fact got a fair trial.

It also occurs to this writer that one might be entitled to wonder why none of the appeal justices were interviewed[82]. In particular, to my mind, the CCA's judgment (293 paragraphs) was far more persuasive than Whealy J's one-liner on a television show. The CCA justices were the judicial officers who had to bear down and articulate reasons, the latter being something that Whealy J has never done. If nothing else, Whealy J was simply mistaken in his uncertainty, in my respectful opinion.

In conclusion, Whealy J's possible doubt about Keli's guilt was of no relevance or importance. In my respectful opinion, it would have been preferable for him to refrain from entering the fray.

Claim 6 – Narelle McCartney (a friend of Keli) was not called by the Crown to give evidence to the jury and, if she had been called, she would have said Keli told her about an "Andrew", thereby corroborating Keli on his existence. Accordingly, the jury would have entertained doubt about Keli's guilt[83]

Ms McCartney was interviewed by *Exposed* and stated that Keli had told her about meeting "Andrew" and having an affair with him[84]. Ms McCartney said she had told police about this.

---

[82] I have, of course, assumed they were not asked by *Exposed* for interviews. My comment can be disregarded if they were in fact asked. By the term "appeals" in this sentence, I mean the appeal to the CCA and the application for special leave to appeal to the HCA.

[83] *Exposed*, Episode 3, at 0.45. At the outset, there might be several threshold questions about the admissibility of this evidence were it ever sought to be tendered at a trial. However, for present purposes, I will overlook these matters, and assume, in Keli's favour, and in *Exposed's* favour, that the evidence would be admissible.

[84] Ms McCartney was one friend of Keli who had not given evidence at the inquest in 2005/06.

There were a number of problems with this claim. Ms McCartney certainly had been interviewed by police. And she had signed a statement. But there was nothing said in that statement about Keli having mentioned "Andrew". Therefore, it seems doubtful that Ms McCartney told police about the conversation. This makes Ms McCartney's claim about the conversation appear unreliable or untruthful. The Crown does not have to call witnesses who are unreliable or untruthful[85].

The problems with Ms McCartney's potential evidence did not end there. She actually was called to give evidence on the *voir dire*. A *voir dire* is an interlocutory (in this case preliminary) hearing of evidence. Ms McCartney's *voir dire* evidence was given on 3 August 2010, in advance of the jury being empanelled (which was to happen on 9 August). The hearing of evidence in this way may be undertaken for any number of forensic or logistical reasons[86]. Although the evidence is given in the context of the trial, it does not normally form part of the evidence that the jury hears or considers.

I have read the transcript of Ms McCartney's evidence on the *voir dire*. During the Crown's cross-examination a number of matters arose that were, in my opinion, plainly adverse to her credibility. Furthermore, Ms McCartney became evasive and argumentative, which damaged her credibility even further. When this is added to Ms McCartney's failure to mention the conversation with Keli in her police statement, it becomes clear, I think, that the Crown had good reason to view Ms McCartney's evidence as untruthful and unreliable. Accordingly, the Crown had no obligation to call Ms McCartney to testify to the jury.

There was another matter that made Ms McCartney's claim of Keli mentioning "Andrew" even less credible - Keli herself had never said anything about it. When asked by Gaut in 2002 whether any of her friends might know "Andrew", Keli mentioned nothing of Ms McCartney knowing of him. And when asked by Kehoe in

---

[85] Rule 88 of the Bar Rules.
[86] Here there were primarily logistical reasons. It is unnecessary to set out those reasons.

2001, Keli said things consistent with Ms McCartney not knowing of "Andrew" or not having been around when she, Keli, was having her alleged affair with "Andrew". *Exposed* did not inform its audience of this evidence.

In my opinion, it has to be inferred from all of this that, in truth, there had been no conversation between Keli and Ms McCartney about "Andrew". The conversation was invented later.

Exposed also omitted to mention that neither party had exclusive rights to interview or call Ms McCartney to testify. Thus, it was open to Keli to call Ms McCartney to testify to the jury if she wished. She elected not to call Ms McCartney. It has to be supposed that Keli and her lawyers formed the same view about the unreliability of Ms McCartney as the Crown.

Finally, Keli said nothing about Ms McCartney not testifying to the jury when she, Keli, appealed to the CCA[87]. Keli's appeal was her opportunity to ventilate her concerns about the trial. She was represented in the appeal by two counsel. It can be inferred that Keli received sound advice about how to conduct her appeal and which matters generated arguable complaints about the trial. But nothing was said about Ms McCartney or the Crown's omission to call Ms McCartney. *Exposed* did not mention to its audience that Keli had said nothing about Ms McCartney in her appeal.

In summary, almost certainly, Ms McCartney's evidence was not tendered to the jury by Keli or the Crown because both parties considered it untruthful, unreliable and of no assistance. I consider there were clearly legitimate reasons for both parties to refrain from calling Ms McCartney to testify to the jury. Any suggestion that Ms McCartney ought to have been called as a witness by either party or that her evidence would have altered the outcome of the trial can be disregarded.

---

[87] *Lane v. R* [2013] NSWCCA 317.

Claim 7(a) – A witness whose name really was Andrew Morris was "coached" or "led" by the Crown to give false evidence.
Claim 7(b) – A "deal" was done to keep the real Andrew Morris (and Ms McCartney) from giving evidence;

These claims might appear, at first blush, inconsistent with each other, and they were. But that did not deter *Exposed* from advancing them.

Episode 3 of *Exposed* saw an attempt to convey that a man whose name really was Andrew Morris (I shall refer to him as "AM1") had been "coached" or "led" by police into signing a statement to the effect he had had a sexual encounter with Keli at a northern Sydney beach.

By way of background, AM1 was one of a number of men identified by police throughout Australia who were of relevant age and had the name "Andrew Morris". He did not have Tegan and he had never been the father of Tegan. He explained to *Exposed* that he was called in by detectives for an interview and shown a photo of a group of young people which included Keli. The detective/s asked *"well how do you know her?"*. AM1 answered: *"I don't know, I can't remember, she just looks familiar"*[88].

AM1 then explained to *Exposed* that he was supplied with further details by the police and he formed the opinion that Keli was the girl with whom he had had a sexual encounter:

> *"With the information that I was then provided by the police like they told me she grew up in the northern suburbs of Sydney, they told me that she was a groupie following all the surf club competitions, made me think well, oh, it must have been her, it must have been Keli Lane"* [sic] [89]

AM1 signed a police statement in which he purported to identify Keli in the photographs. AM1's evidence was potentially helpful to the Crown and harmful to Keli. It had the potential to disprove Keli's

---

[88] *Exposed*, Episode 3, at 0.43.
[89] *Exposed*, Episode 3, at 0.43.

account of giving Tegan to an "Andrew Morris" - here was an "Andrew Morris", who it could be inferred was the "Andrew Morris" who had slept with Keli, and he did not have Tegan.

Pausing there, there was nothing remarkable about the gathering of this evidence from AM1. He was initially unsure of his identification of Keli (not unusual). Police have "led" him by giving him some details about Keli (not unusual, and hardly improper in the context of signing a statement). He has considered that information and come to the view that it "*must have been Keli*". This hardly seems remarkable. There does not seem to have been any undue cajoling by the police. It appeared AM1 came to his final stated position of his own free will. He did not appear on camera to be under any legal incapacity (under age or mentally incapable). He appeared healthy and intelligent, aged possibly in his 30s or early 40s. He was light hearted and smiled during the interview. He made a clapping motion and sound near the start of the filmed scene apparently in jest with the camera crew. It did not look like recall of the events was causing him anxiety nor that he perceived there was anything untoward done by anybody. All in all, he looked quite pleased with himself[90]. AM1 might be the only person in the recent history of criminal litigation in Australia who has found the whole experience of a police interview rather pleasant and the source of some mirth and merriment.

Having said that, plainly AM1's identification of Keli was not very convincing. It seems doubtful that the Crown would have been confident about the prospects of the jury accepting it. In any event, all of this became academic when, shortly before the trial commenced, it emerged that, for various reasons, AM1's beach sexual encounter could not possibly have been with Keli. Therefore, AM1's evidence was irrelevant. What followed, as best as I can interpret events, was that the question of whether AM1 was to give evidence to the jury was left in abeyance whilst discussions were undertaken between the parties. There was nothing unusual or untoward about this.

---

[90] *Exposed*, Episode 3, at 0.42.

Ultimately, and I think predictably, agreement was reached between Keli's lawyers and the Crown that AM1 was not to be called to give evidence to the jury.

Notwithstanding the irrelevance of AM1's evidence, and the fact that he would never testify to the jury, *Exposed* sought to make out a case that the police had sought to improperly influence him to give evidence. In a later segment of the interview with AM1, he stated the following to the reporter:

"I suppose I was led down to believe [Keli was the girl] I slept with"[91]

Ms Rhodes was again interviewed and this time the *Exposed* interviewer introduced the notion that AM1 had been "coached" as well as "led". Amusingly, and ironically, the interviewer herself set about putting leading questions to Ms Rhodes:

"Q.   *Looking back on this now, considering the pressure, can you acknowledge the possibility that [AM1] was led or coached?*
Rhodes   *Yes.*
Q.   *To come up with a memory.*
Rhodes   *Yes I can see that in hindsight, yes I can. I don't like admitting that but yeah I can see that"*[92]

At the outset, coaching is not the same as leading. The term "coaching" implies some form of instruction to a witness as to how the witness should testify (i.e. what the witness should say). I have not seen any evidence in this case from which an inference of coaching a witness could be drawn. Even AM1 himself did not say anything giving rise to an inference that he was coached. An allegation of coaching is a serious allegation. It would be expected to be based upon suitably serious and

---

[91] *Exposed,* Episode 3, at 0.47.
[92] *Exposed,* Episode 3, at 0.48.

unambiguous evidence[93]. Far from that, the allegation appears not to have been based upon any evidence at all.

Leading typically occurs when the answer to a question is suggested in the question itself, or where there is some form of guiding or assisting the witness in stating his or her recollection. True there was, it appears, in one form or another, some leading of AM1 in the preparation of his statement. But it was mild, and not improper. In any event, leading is not prohibited in the formulation of a statement[94]. And all of this was of no consequence because AM1 would never testify to the jury.

I am mystified as to why *Exposed* would advance against the police a case of coaching or leading a person who did not, ultimately, give evidence. Presumably only the producers of the documentary would know why this was done.

The next development was a resumption of the interview with Ms McCartney:

> "Q.   *Do you have any idea why you weren't called as a witness?*
>
> Ms McCartney   *No*"[95]

The *Exposed* interviewer told Ms McCartney she had been "*traded out in a witness swap [for AM1]*"[96]. Then Dr Ruyters was reintroduced and made this comment:

> "*The deal was that [Ms McCartney] wouldn't be called in exchange for [AM1] not being called . . . part of the game playing*

---

[93] *Briginshaw v. Briginshaw* (1938) 60 CLR 336. This is the legal standard. It also represents common sense. It is submitted that the public is entitled to expect the same standard of investigative journalism.

[94] Whealy J happened to address this very point in one of his interlocutory judgments in respect of another witness, Ms Townsend, who was unable to recall matters which featured in a statement signed by her: " . . . *statements made to police are not outpourings of a witness as to their recollection. Witnesses are sometimes, within proper limits, guided, assisted and prompted as to their recollection. I do not suggest for one minute that there is anything unfair in that process, or inappropriate. It is simply the way it sometimes happens. So statements appear that, upon careful and appropriate cross examination, cannot be sustained in the witness' recollection*": *R v. Lane [No. 1]* [2010] NSWSC 1528, at paragraph 8.

[95] *Exposed*, Episode 3, at 0.48.

[96] *Exposed*, Episode 3, at 0.48. It was not at all clear to me what exactly was meant by the term "*witness swap*". On no view of the events were any witnesses actually "swapped".

*that goes on during the trial process I think there's an enormous lot
that the public doesn't know about the game playing"*[97]

The *"witness swap"* and *"game playing"* were apparently references to
the *"deal"*. The *"deal"* seems to have been an agreement between the
parties to dispense with the evidence of Ms McCartney and AM1.
However, as we have seen, the evidence of each witness was, for one
reason or another, of no use. It was hardly surprising, or deserving
of characterisation as *"game playing"*, that an agreement was reached
between parties to not take up the jury's time with such witnesses. The
real reason for Ms McCartney not being called to testify to the jury
was <u>not</u> that she was *"traded out in a witness swap"*. The real reason
was, almost certainly, that she was adjudged untruthful and unreliable
by both parties.

Then Ms Rhodes again:

"Q: *If the jury didn't hear from everyone they should have,
          what does that make the trial?*
Rhodes: *I think it's not fair. The jury needs to hear from
          everybody"*[98]

It was not made clear whether Ms Rhodes was directing her
comments towards the defence counsel (Chapple SC) for his
omission to call Ms McCartney to testify to the jury or, on the
other hand, the Crown for his omission to call AM1 to testify to
the jury. If Ms Rhodes was directing herself to the defence counsel,
she was mistaken. There was no obligation upon defence counsel
to call all witnesses or evidence in his possession. If Ms Rhodes was
directing herself to the Crown, she was equally incorrect, but for
different reasons. The situation was governed by the Bar Rules which
provided, relevantly, as follows:

---

[97] *Exposed*, Episode 3, at 0.47 and at 0.49.
[98] *Exposed*, Episode 3, at 0.49.

> "82.   *A prosecutor must place the whole of the <u>relevant</u> evidence before the court.*
>
> 88.   *A prosecutor must call as part of the prosecution's case all witnesses whose testimony is admissible and <u>necessary</u> unless the <u>defence counsel consents</u> to the prosecutor not calling a particular witness . . ."* [emphasis added]

The defence counsel consented to AM1 not being called. Even if that was incorrect, the Crown would have been entitled to regard AM1 as not relevant or necessary. Therefore, the Crown had no obligation to call AM1.

Ultimately, it was the Crown's decision as to which witnesses were to be called for the prosecution, and the Crown's decision alone[99]. My view is that there could not be any controversy about the Crown's omission to call AM1. It is not hard to imagine the chaos that would reign in the criminal justice system if the law did not assign the Crown the discretion about which witnesses ought to be called for the prosecution. Trials would be longer and more expensive and juries would become distracted by irrelevant or unnecessary witnesses, and so on. There was no basis for calling into question the Crown's decision as to which witnesses were called to give evidence to the jury.

In conclusion:

1. there was no coaching of AM1;
2. whatever leading of AM1 took place was minor and inconsequential;
3. the evidence of AM1 was irrelevant and unnecessary;
4. neither counsel had an obligation to call AM1 (or Ms McCartney);
5. there was no *"witness swap"*; and
6. once the facts are fully known and properly understood, it can be seen there was nothing in the interviews with

---

[99] *Lane v. R* [2013] NSWCCA 317 at paragraph 164; *Richardson v. Queen* [1974] HCA 19; 131 CLR 116 at 120-121.

AM1, Ms McCartney or Ms Rhodes that provided reason to doubt the fairness of the trial or soundness of the conviction.

Claim 8 – Keli has been prevented from telling her side of the story[100]

This claim was articulated in terms of *"the defence"* not calling Keli to give evidence, creating the impression that Keli wanted to give evidence but her lawyers somehow denied her that right.

The ordinary course of events in the lawyer/client relationship is that the lawyer gives advice to the client, the client then elects whether or not to follow that advice, and then the client instructs the lawyer what course s/he wishes to take. The lawyer is, first and foremost, an advisor[101]. Absent anything proved to the contrary, it is safe to assume that the relationship between Keli and her lawyers followed the usual course. I am unaware of anything tending to establish that the usual course was not followed. Therefore, on the question of whether Keli was to give evidence, it is safe to assume that the lawyers rendered advice, that Keli made her own election and that her election was to not give evidence.

It would certainly be improper for the lawyers to somehow deny Keli the right to give evidence in circumstances where she wanted to do so. If that were the case, one might expect to see a complaint by Keli to that effect in the CCA, but no such complaint was made. It can be safely assumed the lawyers did not improperly constrain Keli from giving evidence.

It can probably be inferred in the circumstances of the case that the lawyers' advice to Keli was against giving evidence. I think it would be the advice of most lawyers. One important consideration was that the defendant generally bears no onus of proving anything in her defence. Another consideration against Keli giving evidence was her history

---

[100] *Exposed*, Episode 3, at 0.49.

[101] There are some matters in respect of which a barrister is entitled to make the call without advising the client or seeking the client's instructions, but these matters are not relevant to this discussion.

of mendacity. It would be surprising, with that history, if she was to survive cross-examination with any credibility.

In any event, the jury was hardly deprived of Keli's side of the story. Her side was spilled out in lengthy videotaped interviews and documents which the jury saw and heard.

In summary, Keli has never been prevented by anybody from telling her side of the story.

Claim 9 – Contrary to the Crown's case, Keli was in fact discharged from Auburn Hospital at 2.00pm on 14 September 1996 and arrived home at Fairlight at 3.00pm. This did not allow her enough time to murder Tegan and dispose of Tegan's body. Therefore, the Crown did not prove Keli had an opportunity to murder Tegan[102]

That Keli was discharged at 2.00pm was not accepted by the jury. It was not even raised by Keli in the CCA, which suggests Keli herself disavowed it (which she in fact did, as will be seen below).

The claim was developed by *Exposed* in the following way. First, the Auburn Hospital records were shown on camera. They revealed an entry comprising a note apparently made at 1400 hrs (2.00pm) about the discharge of Keli (with Tegan). This note had been made by a Registered Nurse Ann Hanlon ("RN Hanlon"). It was not clear whether the note was intended to signify that the discharge actually occurred at 1400 hrs or, on the other hand, merely that the note was made at 1400 hrs. It was stated that RN Hanlon declined to be interviewed for the program.

There were a number of other matters written into the 1400 hrs entry by RN Hanlon, for example a conversation with a doctor who apparently approved Keli's discharge, a process of transferral of Keli to the RDMP, postnatal observations, a finding about the *"uterus involuting appropriately"*, and so on and so forth. By my count, there

---

[102] *Exposed*, Episode 3, at 0.31.

were some eight, possibly nine, separate matters contained in the 1400 hrs entry[103].

Viewers were then shown a statement signed by RN Hanlon and dated 14 August 2003 in which the nurse had stated *"Keli Lane and her child were discharged around 14.00 hours"* (2.00pm).

Viewers were then shown a subsequent statement by RN Hanlon signed in 2008 in which she stated that Keli left the hospital between 11.00am and 12.00pm[104].

A Dr Stephen Chen was interviewed:

> *"If she did leave at 12.00 noon then nursing staff should have reported she left at 12.00 noon. I was the senior medical officer on the ward that day. [The time I think according to these notes that Keli Lane was discharged from the hospital was] within an hour after 2"*[105]

In this way, *Exposed* developed a seemingly powerful argument to the effect that Keli was discharged from the hospital at 2.00pm. However, *Exposed* omitted to mention the following matters.

First, the only time that Keli herself has spoken about the time of her departure from Auburn Hospital was when she was interviewed by Kehoe (in 2001) and said she left *"before 12.00 o'clock sometime"*[106].

---

[103] *Exposed,* Episode 3, at 0.35.

[104] *Exposed,* Episode 3, at 0.33.

[105] *Exposed,* Episode 3, at 0.34.

[106] I have seen questioning of the value of Keli's statement given that she was an admitted liar, and a prolific one at that. However, a history of mendacity, even one as severe as Keli's history, does not necessarily mean that every single utterance by the witness in question is to be disbelieved. It does mean that extra care must be exercised before anything said by the witness is accepted. This often translates into acceptance of such a witness's statements where they are, for example, corroborated by other evidence. Keli's statement, in this instance, was corroborated by Ms Duraisamy. For this reason alone, it was likely truthful. Another circumstance in which a statement by such a witness might be believed is where the witness is making an admission against interest. Admissions against interest are such highly probative pieces of evidence that they cannot be disregarded just because the witness is otherwise, or generally, not to be believed. Keli's statement was an admission against interest. This was another reason to consider it truthful. I am also persuaded to this view by the fact that the way in which Keli made the statement was relatively spontaneous and it appears credible when one reads it in the context of the whole of the interview. The same cannot be said about many of the other statements made by Keli to Kehoe (and Gaut).

Furthermore, another patient on the ward, a Ms Duraisamy, would later give evidence to the effect that she woke before 11.00am and Keli and Tegan were gone by then[107]. This was the best evidence about when Keli departed. RN Hanlon never claimed to have witnessed Keli's departure. To the extent there was conflict between, on the one hand, the statement of Keli and evidence of Ms Duraisamy and, on the other hand, the evidence of RN Hanlon, the jurors would have been entitled to wholly disregard the latter's note, and they may well have done so. Put simply, on one strong view of it, RN Hanlon's note (and first statement) was immaterial and inconsequential.

Alternatively, taking into account the evidence of Keli and Ms Duraisamy, the jury would have been entitled to accept RN Hanlon's second (2008) statement. As the HCA stated in the Lindy Chamberlain case:

> "At the end of the trial the jury must consider all the evidence, and in doing so they may find that one piece of evidence resolves their doubts as to another. For example, the jury, considering the evidence of one witness by itself, may doubt whether it is truthful, but other evidence may provide corroboration, and when the jury considers the evidence as a whole they may decide that the witness should be believed"[108]

For these reasons, with or without RN Hanlon's evidence, it was beyond question that Keli left the hospital at the latest by 12.00 midday.

The vice in the argument as it was developed by *Exposed* was that RN Hanlon was (wrongly) promoted to the status of being the most important Crown witness on the topic. Viewers were then misled into thinking that, because there was ambiguity about her evidence, there

---

[107] I have been unable to source the transcript of Ms Duraisamy's evidence. Newspaper reports of her evidence described her as saying Keli was gone by 11.00am. The CCA would later note Keli's departure as occurring between 11.00am and 12.00 midday : *R v. Lane* [2013] NSWCCA 317 at paragraph 195. I think it is fair to assume Keli's departure was between 11.00am and 12.00 midday.

[108] *Chamberlain v The Queen [No 2]* [1984] HCA 7; (1984) 153 CLR 521.

must have been uncertainty about the Crown's case. In truth, RN Hanlon's evidence was of little or no importance at all.

Secondly, it would be a strange confluence of events if all of the eight or nine matters recorded in RN Hanlon's entry actually occurred simultaneously at 2.00pm, as seems to be the logic of the contention advanced by *Exposed*. It defies belief, frankly. It follows that some of those matters must have occurred before 2.00pm. Of itself, this does not mean Keli's departure occurred before 2.00pm. But it generates even more comfort about the evidence of Keli and Ms Duraisamy.

Thirdly, as we have seen, Keli was in a hurry to leave the hospital on Saturday 14 September, so much so that she did not get around to the Guthrie test or identification procedures that were supposed to be undertaken. This does not prove conclusively that she left before 12.00 midday, but it is inconsistent with her having hung around until 2.00pm.

Fourthly, Keli never complained to the CCA about anything in connection with the hospital departure time. If there was real reason to find that she left at 2.00pm, it would be expected that Keli would have said something to that effect in her appeal. It would have been something of a game changer that would have raised a serious question about the conviction. But Keli and her lawyers said nothing[109].

Before leaving discussion of RN Hanlon, it is worth noting that there was not anything necessarily sinister or remarkable about the inconsistency between her 2003 and 2008 statements. There could be a number of valid explanations. As Whealy J said "*statements made to police are not outpourings of a witness as to their recollection*"[110]. To get this into context, the first statement (2003) was made and signed for the purposes of the Coronial inquests in 2004 and 2005/06. In my experience, these statements are often drafted and signed in a somewhat perfunctory manner. It is not unusual to see changes in statements. It is not unusual to see inconsistencies. These things do

[109] *Lane v. R* [2013] NSWCCA 317.
[110] *R v. Lane [No. 1]* [2010] NSWSC 1628, at paragraph 8.

not always mean the witness is not to be believed. Sometimes they do, sometimes they don't. The remedy for the person against whom the evidence is tendered (in this case Keli) is that she has the opportunity to cross-examine and thereby test the witness. It was then up to the jury to watch and listen to the cross-examination and assess the truthfulness and reliability of RN Hanlon's evidence in conjunction with the other evidence on the topic. It is impossible to conceive of any prejudice to Keli.

It remains to deal with the statements of Dr Chen. To recap, the first sentence of his "evidence" on *Exposed* was this: *"If she did leave at 12.00 noon then nursing staff should have reported she left at 12.00 noon"*.

There are numerous problems with Dr Chen's statement. First, I have spoken to several experienced nurses during this project who have told me that nurses do not, as a matter of standard nursing practice or as a routine, write up notes of events contemporaneously. Furthermore, for what it is worth, the timing of nursing notes was an issue that arose from time to time in cases I conducted. I interviewed, examined and cross-examined a number of nurses about this very subject. I cannot recall a nurse ever saying it was standard practice to write up all notes contemporaneously, especially when the notes pertain to something as unremarkable as the patient departing the hospital.

Secondly, even if Dr Chen's statement was correct, all that it established was that RN Hanlon might have departed from accepted standards of nursing practice in the way in which she wrote up notes. It fell short of establishing that RN Hanlon was in fact not to be believed on her assertion that Keli's departure actually occurred at or before midday.

The second sentence of Dr Chen's "evidence" was that, on the basis of the entry at 2.00pm, he thought Keli was discharged *"within an hour after 2"*. Pausing there, generally speaking, the law is slow to attach evidentiary weight to one person's opinion, or thoughts, about what another person intends to convey when the latter makes or records a statement. This has always seemed to me a sensible stricture, and one that arises for obvious reasons. RN Hanlon plainly did not intend by her entry in the notes to convey that Keli actually left at 2.00pm. Dr Chen was simply not in a position to gainsay RN Hanlon about this. In the result, nothing said by Dr Chen was reason to doubt that Keli was discharged by 12.00 midday at the latest.

Dr Chen's "evidence" on *Exposed* was infected with the fundamental difficulty that it was only evidence about what he thought about an event (not having seen or experienced the event himself). Such evidence ought not normally prevail over evidence from witnesses who saw or experienced the event such as Keli and Ms Duraisamy.

Finally, it is not known what information Dr Chen was provided with in advance of his interview with *Exposed*. It has to be wondered what he would say if he was fully acquainted with the matters I have set out. It seems unlikely he would say what he said in the face of knowledge that Keli herself and another witness had stated Keli left before 12.00 midday. Likewise, it has to be wondered what Dr Chen would make of Keli's failure to complain about the jury's finding in the CCA.

For all of these reasons, *Exposed's* claim that Keli was not discharged until 2.00pm on 14 September 1996 can safely be disregarded.

Claim 10 – The false swearing charges should not have been heard together with the murder charge. The joinder of the false swearing and murder charges unfairly prejudiced Keli's defence[111]

This argument was presented by Keli in the CCA, and unanimously rejected. The CCA dealt with it on the relatively simple, but nonetheless compelling, basis that Keli elected, through her lawyers, to

---

[111] *Exposed*, Episode 3, at 0.18.

consent to the joinder. But there were other equally compelling reasons that this claim makes little sense.

Exposed appeared to gain support for the claim from Dr Ruyters who said the following:

> *"[The joinder of the false swearing and murder charges] was incredibly damaging for Keli because . . . [T]he only case [the Crown] could make was one that they constructed around the lies that Keli had told on the adoption papers. That opened the door to her previous sexual history, all of the previous pregnancies and associated lies that she told when she wanted to hide what was happening to her from her family and friends and the nett effect of that was that this put Keli up as this progressive liar "* [sic][112]

In my view, this statement was misconceived. The adoption papers (by which I take Dr Ruyters to mean the Supreme Court affidavits[113]) did not, by themselves, open the door to the material that proved Keli's sexual history and history of lying. There were also the papers of the eight other agencies previously listed. All of this material (the adoption papers and the other papers) went into evidence on numerous bases, namely background, credibility and tendency in the murder charge. Part of the material also went in as evidence of consciousness of guilt (for murder) – directly relevant to her guilt for murder. The admission of none of this material depended upon the false swearing charges being heard with the murder charge. The material was admitted into evidence on the murder charge, and would have been so admitted on the murder charge irrespective of whether the false swearing charges were being heard at the same time.

Explicit proof that the lies were admitted into evidence on the murder charge, if proof be needed, can be found in statements made

---

[112] Ibid, at 0.19.

[113] They were displayed on camera as Dr Ruyters spoke. Even if this assumption is incorrect, the analysis which follows remains the same.

by Whealy J and the CCA during the course of the trial. The following examples will suffice:

1. On 23 August, in the course of delivering an interlocutory judgment, Whealy J specifically described the lies surrounding the births of Trisha and Archie as "*lies going to credibility and background in the murder charge*"[114].
2. On 6 October, Whealy J confirmed in another interlocutory judgment that the lies sought to be admitted as tendency evidence on the murder charge were already before the jury as background and credibility evidence in the murder charge[115].
3. On 3 November, Whealy J confirmed that the lies in general were admissible on credibility and some of them were admissible as tendency evidence, as he had earlier ruled[116]. All of this was plainly referable to the murder charge.
4. On 16 November (reasons for judgment published on 14 July 2011), the CCA noted there was "*no issue that the evidence of the statements said to have been made by [Keli] was admissible*"[117]. This statement was plainly referable to the murder charge (the murder charge was the only subject of the appeal).
5. In another interlocutory judgment delivered on 17 November, Whealy J made it plain the lies were in evidence in the murder charge[118].
6. After the trial, on 13 December 2013, the CCA said:
    "*The other false statements [besides the three admitted as evidence of consciousness of guilt] . . . were relevant to the*

---

[114] *R v. Lane [no. 5]* [2010] NSWSC 1523, at paragraph 11.
[115] *R v. Lane [No.11]* [2010] NSWSC 1538 at paragraph 14.
[116] *R v. Lane [No.14]* [2010] NSWSC 1541 at paragraphs 5, 13 and 39.
[117] *R v. Lane* [2011] NSWCCA 157, per Simpson J at paragraph 32.
[118] *R v. Lane [No.18]* [2010] NSWSC 1545 at paragraph 10.

> *assessment of [Keli's] credibility. This had particular poignancy because, [Keli] not having given evidence in the trial, reliance had to be placed upon what she had previously said"*[119]

It could hardly be clearer that the lies went into evidence on the murder charge. Their admission into evidence was not dependent upon the false swearing charges being heard with the murder charge.

Even if the above is incorrect, Keli's lawyers did not oppose the joinder of the false swearing and murder charges, even when pointedly asked about their position by Whealy J shortly before the trial commenced. Whealy J may well have been expecting Keli's lawyers to oppose the joinder at that stage. Ordinarily, it would be expected that an accused person would not want false swearing charges heard together with a murder charge. But this begs some questions in Keli's case: (1) was it an ordinary case? and (2) to what extent was the jury actually influenced to convict Keli for murder merely because she was a liar?

The answer to the first question was that this was not an ordinary case. The extent of Keli's lying, either proved against or admitted by her, was immense. There was no point in Keli contesting the proposition that she was a chronic liar. Her lies were so immense and mostly so outlandish that she would have looked foolish to the jury if she tried to prove she was not lying. Therefore, Keli's lawyers were basically cornered into conducting the defence not on the basis that Keli was not a liar, but rather on the basis that she should not be convicted of murder for telling lies. That being so, there was little to be gained by severing the false swearing charges from the murder charge. The false swearing charges were, after all, but a drop in the ocean of the overall web of deceit.

---

[119] *Lane v. R* [2013] NSWCCA 317 at paragraph 265.

I turn now to the second question – to what extent, if at all, did the jury convict Keli merely because she was a liar? The answer is that it was most unlikely the jury did so, for the reasons which follow.

First, Whealy J warned the jury that it was impermissible to find Keli guilty of murder merely on the basis that she was a liar. As we have seen, two weeks into the trial there had already been two warnings to the jury about this. It has been estimated that Whealy J delivered no less than 35 separate warnings about the lies to the jury during the four month trial. The operation of the criminal law requires the assumption that, as a general rule, juries follow the directions they are given by the trial judge[120]. That is to say, absent some compelling factor to the contrary, it can be assumed the jury followed Whealy J's directions. There was no factor to the contrary in this case (much less anything compelling). There was never any complaint by Keli in the CCA or the HCA about the terms of the warnings. Nor was there any complaint that the jury convicted her on the basis of merely being a liar or disregarded the directions given by Whealy J[121]. It might be added there were also warnings from Keli's counsel to the same effect. For all of these reasons, it was highly unlikely the jury convicted Keli for murder merely because she was a liar. Neither Dr Ruyters nor *Exposed* appear to have given any thought to this most fundamental of matters – that the jury was (repeatedly) warned about the danger of convicting Keli merely because she was a liar. Certainly *Exposed* said nothing about it to its audience.

Secondly, the jurors swore an oath to determine the case in accordance with the evidence. To conclude they decided Keli's guilt on an impermissible basis would be to find that the jurors betrayed their oath. Such a serious finding would require some serious evidence to that effect[122]. There was no evidence at all.

---

[120] *Gilbert v. R* [2000] HCA 15; 201 CLR 414.

[121] *Lane v. R* [2013] NSWCCA 317.

[122] *Briginshaw v. Briginshaw* (1938) 60 CLR 336.

The fact that Keli's lawyers did not oppose the joinder suggests, at least, that they advised her not to oppose it and that she instructed them accordingly. Absent incompetence on the lawyers' part (about which there was no evidence), Keli was bound by her lawyers' conduct of the case[123]. In effect, after having the benefit of legal advice, Keli elected not to oppose the joinder. In my view, the correct course was taken.

There was an inherent and unusual difficulty in this case, entirely of Keli's making. No matter where the evidence turned, it found lies and half-truths told by Keli. We have already seen how the lies went into evidence as relevant to Keli's credibility, and also for other purposes. It would have been unavoidable in the prosecution of Keli to somehow tiptoe around the lies. The prosecution would be thwarted. It would be an absurd outcome if an accused person could rely upon her own lies to thwart a prosecution.

I have observed during this project much misunderstanding about the significance of Keli's lies in her conviction. That Keli was convicted for murder for being a liar is a slogan advanced by many of Keli's supporters. In fairness to these people, there was perhaps a fine line between the legitimate use of the lies and, on the other hand, the impermissible use of the lies to convict her for murder. However, it was a real distinction and one that was given a lot of attention by Whealy J. There is no reason to suspect that the jurors misapprehended their task. Ultimately, whilst the lies were plainly relevant to Keli's guilt in the ways I have endeavoured to demonstrate (both directly and indirectly), she was not convicted for murder merely because she was a liar.

The slogans, of which there are several variations on the same theme, overlook the different ways in which the lies were characterised, and tendered and admitted into evidence, at the trial. It all rather depends upon the types of lies which are under consideration. Thus, if the lies were the types of lies that, in being told, Keli was acting as

---

[123] *R v. Birks* (1990) 19 NSWLR 677.

if she was guilty, and indeed knew she was guilty, then the jury could reason directly from those lies that she was guilty. Alternatively, having offered an explanation of the circumstances she relied upon to assert her innocence, Keli made her own credibility an issue. It is trite in that circumstance that any lies told by her had to be relevant to, and capable of diminishing, the credibility of her explanation of Tegan's disappearance. This was in turn (indirectly) relevant to guilt.

Keli's lies were available to be drawn in aid of her guilt by virtue of all of these forms of reasoning. But that is a world away from the simplistic notion that she was convicted for murder merely because she was a liar. In other words, it wasn't just that Keli told lies. It was the types of lies she told, in particular in the circumstance that she had put her own credibility in issue.

Another complication was that Whealy J was interviewed on *Exposed* and made statements that were capable of being construed as criticisms of the defence counsel for not seeking to sever the false swearing charges from the murder charge. It is not known whether, and if so to what extent, this interview was edited. Whealy J stated that, by virtue of the joinder, Keli became exposed to a serious attack on her credibility which otherwise would not have been available. In my respectful opinion, the value of these comments was questionable. They were, so it appeared, and indeed had to be, referable to defence counsel's failure to make an application for severance <u>before</u> the trial proper commenced[124]. However, at that stage, it seems doubtful that Whealy J would have had accurate knowledge of the true extent of Keli's lying, nor the prospect that the lies would be admitted into evidence in the murder charge irrespective of whether the charges were severed (which is what eventually happened). Given the way the trial would develop, and the ways in which the lies were ultimately admitted into evidence, it seems inconceivable that Whealy J's comments in *Exposed* can be sensibly interpreted as being other than in the incomplete pre-trial context. That is to say, it is unlikely that it

---

[124] Whealy J actually had invited, or "hinted" to, defence counsel to consider applying for severance of the false swearing charges. This was, of course, before the trial commenced.

was the joinder of the charges, per se, that made possible the attack on Keli's credibility. That attack was always going to happen even in the absence of the false swearing charges.

In fairness to Whealy J, ordinarily a trial judge would not be expected to have much, or any, appreciation of evidence yet to be adduced. But it does mean, I think, that Whealy J's implied criticism of defence counsel was misplaced. This leads to another point. Whealy J cannot have known what was in defence counsel's brief, or what instructions defence counsel had from Keli. In my respectful opinion, the enormity of Keli's lying was good reason for defence counsel to conduct the trial in the way he did[125]. For all of these reasons, it seems to me it was inappropriate of Whealy J to seek to gainsay defence counsel's conduct of the case. And for the reasons previously set out, and as is clear from the way in which the trial actually developed, the joinder of the charges did not expose Keli to a credibility attack that was otherwise unavailable – the credibility attack would have been available with or without the false swearing charges.

Finally, there was probably an additional reason behind Keli's decision to acquiesce in the joinder. Had the trials been separated, and had Keli been acquitted of murder, she would have had to return to court at a later stage to face the false swearing charges. I think it can be safely inferred that this figured in Keli's strategy. She said as much when interviewed by *Exposed*, commenting to the effect that it was better to get all the charges over and done with together.

For all of these reasons, Dr Ruyters' comments ought to be disregarded and Whealy J's comments can also be disregarded when understood in the context that he appears to have been talking about events prior to the trial proper actually commencing. Alternatively, Whealy J was in no position to gainsay the defence counsel's conduct

---

[125] Indeed, it might have been difficult for defence counsel to run any other defence given that Mr Hamill SC had conceded Keli's deceit at the Coronial inquest back in 2005. This should not be understood as a criticism of Mr Hamill SC in any way, shape or form. In my opinion, Mr Hamill SC's concession was one that had to be made.

of the trial. It would have been pointless, and even positively unwise, to sever the false swearing and murder charges.

Claim 11 – When Detective Kehoe called Keli in to Manly Police Station in February 2001 for an interview, he was "casual" and made it out to be a "custody issue". Thus, Keli did not understand the seriousness of the interview and did not think she needed a lawyer present[126]

In my view, suspicion must attach to Keli's claims that Kehoe was "*casual*" and made out that the interview related to custody matters. Mr Borovnik (DOCS) had made it clear to Keli in 1999 that he suspected foul play and he was referring the matter to the police. It was unlikely that Keli was left under any misapprehension about DOCS' interest in Tegan, or that its concern was limited to a custody issue. There was, of course, no custody issue. And Kehoe prefaced his interview in 2001 with a clear statement that he was investigating the whereabouts of Tegan, together with the usual warning that whatever was said might be used against Keli in evidence. It was unlikely Keli was under any illusions about the interview.

There were more problems with this claim about the interview with Kehoe. As a general rule, a person needs a lawyer present at a police interview principally to ensure that the person does not confess to a crime without being informed and educated about his/her right to silence. If Keli had confessed murder to Kehoe, then the absence of a lawyer may have been significantly prejudicial. But that did not happen. Instead, Keli set out, reasonably stoutly, the defence she would maintain through until the end of her trial and beyond: that she had given baby Tegan to "Andrew Morris/Norris". It can hardly be said that anything prejudicial was occasioned to Keli by virtue of the absence of a lawyer.

I have given consideration to whether Keli might have been better off staying silent when interviewed by Kehoe. However, for the reasons

---

[126] *Exposed*, Episode 2, at 0.18ff, 0.24.

that follow, I have come to the view that maintenance of silence would not necessarily have assisted Keli and may have even caused additional harm to her defence. There is an exception to the general rules about the accused's right to silence and the Crown's onus of proof. In the case of *Weissensteiner v. R*, the HCA held that where the accused is peculiarly in a position to shed light on what is otherwise a mystery, then an adverse inference may be drawn against the accused if he or she fails to give evidence[127]. If Keli did not speak to the police, and give the "Andrew Morris/Norris" explanation, she might have found herself obliged to assist with solving the mystery at the trial by giving evidence. This would be a parlous situation for Keli because, frankly, it was unlikely her story would survive cross-examination. If I am right, it can be seen that it may well have been better for Keli to proffer her story at the police station rather than offering it up at the trial with a Crown prosecutor breathing down her neck.

For all of these reasons, the absence of a lawyer when Keli was interviewed by Kehoe was of no consequence.

Claim 12 – The searches for "Andrew" and Tegan were never completed by the police

Whealy J was interviewed by *Exposed* and commented that the police searches "*should have been completed*" before the trial began.

I am unaware of any requirement that the Crown prove its searches were "complete". Given that the searches were ostensibly seeking to prove a negative (i.e. that Tegan was not deceased), it might reasonably be questioned whether it was logically possible to "complete" such searches. It is a source of curiosity to this writer as to what would have constituted "completion". As the Coroner stated: "*it is difficult to imagine that any search could be exhaustive*"[128].

The interviewer and Whealy J appear to have been at cross purposes. Having re-watched the interview several times, it appears to

---

[127] *Weissensteiner v. R* (1993) 178 CLR 217; (1993) HCA 65; see also *The Queen v Baden-Clay* (2016) 258 CLR 308; *RPS v The Queen* (2000) 199 CLR 620 at 633.

[128] Coronial findings 15 February 2006.

me Whealy J was talking about the "completeness" of investigations in the sense of procedural completion by the prosecution of its preparation for trial. There is no doubt, in a procedural sense, the prosecution should have its case ready for trial by the appointed trial date. However, the interviewer was, I think, actually referring to substantive "completion" of the search for Tegan (something which was a logical impossibility). At the very least, *Exposed* left this topic in a confused state.

The alleged incompleteness of the searches was of no consequence so far as concerned the jury's task of determining guilt. The jury's substantive task was to determine whether the searches were <u>sufficient</u> to be probative of the question of whether Tegan was deceased, irrespective of whether they had been "completed". The jury was ultimately satisfied about the sufficiency of the searches. Whealy J himself observed during the trial that the evidence of the searches was *"very extensive"*[129]. The Coroner had earlier described Gaut's investigation up to 2005 alone as *"lengthy, thorough (so far as an investigation essentially trying to prove a negative can be) and time-consuming"*[130]. The CCA described the overall police investigation as, variously, *"comprehensive"*, *"exemplary"*, *"meticulous"*, *"painstaking"*, *"very careful"*, *"thorough"*, *"detailed"* and *"very extensive"*[131]. It is hard, if not impossible, to imagine how the investigation could have been better. Ms Rhodes described the searches as *"massive"* and *"mammoth"* when interviewed on *Exposed*[132]. The CCA concluded that the police investigation *"virtually excluded any possibility that there existed a man named Andrew Morris/Norris with whom [Keli] had had a 'brief affair'"*[133].

Exposed also attempted to discredit the police investigation in another way. Viewers were told that because the police did not start investigating the Wisbeach apartments until 2003, they missed records

---

[129] *R v. Lane [No. 18]* [2010] NSWSC 1545, at paragraph 13.
[130] Coronial findings 15 February 2006.
[131] *Lane v. R* [2013] NSWCCA 317.
[132] *Exposed,* Episode 3, at 0.25.
[133] *Lane v. R* [2013] NSWCCA 317 at paragraph 281.

of tenants and owners before 20 December 1995 (such records having been destroyed before 2003). Keli then told *Exposed* that she had started seeing "Andrew" in September/October 1995[134]. The implication was that the police search was deficient because it missed the period September to November 1995. But there was a major difficulty with this implication. Back in 2001, Keli had told Kehoe that she first met "Andrew" in December 1995. *Exposed's* viewers were not told about this statement. Either Keli was lying when she told *Exposed* it was September/October, or her memory failed her[135]. Either way, the most sensible inference was that Keli met "Andrew" for the first time in December 1995. This coincided with the start date of the police searches for the existence of "Andrew Morris/Norris" at Wisbeach. Therefore, the police search of Wisbeach was not deficient as alleged, or at all[136]. Indeed, the searches would be best described as being reasonably successful in so far as they located Mr Greaves and the Clark brothers in units 10 and 11 respectively.

The next stop in *Exposed's* apparent quest to discredit the police investigation was Dr Ruyters who stated: "*then there's a witness who remembered seeing mail that was addressed to an Andrew Norris*"[137]. This was presumably a reference to the occupant of unit 11, Peter Clark (previously discussed), who claimed to have seen mail to "Andrew Morris" and "Andrew Norris" sitting on top of the unit 10 mail box (Mr Greaves' mail box). *Exposed's* viewers were not told that Mr Clark had given at least two, possibly three, inconsistent versions of his evidence and was discredited at the trial when cross-examined by the Crown[138]. Nor were viewers told that Mr Clark's evidence was

---

[134] *Exposed,* Episode 2, at 0.28.

[135] If it was a memory problem, it is trite to say that her memory of events occurring in 1995 was better when interviewed by Kehoe (2001) than it was when interviewed by *Exposed* (2018).

[136] In any event, it was not until May 2003 that Keli first identified Wisbeach to the police (or anybody). It was Keli herself who made it impossible for police to investigate Wisbeach before destruction of the records in 2003.

[137] *Exposed,* Episode 2, at 0.31

[138] *Lane v. R* [2013] NSWCCA 317 at paragraphs 144 to 169. This cross-examination was undertaken pursuant to leave granted to the Crown under section 38 of the *Evidence Act 1995* (NSW).

described by the CCA as of dubious, or no, value[139]. In conclusion, Mr Clark's evidence can, and should, be ignored.

There was also a suggestion by Dr Ruyters that the police failed to take account of the possibility that "Andrew Morris/Norris" was a sub-tenant. This was another error. The possibility of a sub-tenancy was in fact addressed. Evidence was given at the inquest in 1995 by the real estate agent, a Mr Klein (of Ray White Real Estate) who handled the leasing of every unit at Wisbeach. Mr Klein testified that whilst not all prospective renters had to enter into the lease, nonetheless all had to fill out a tenancy application and show proof of identity. Mr Klein conceded the possibility of somebody moving in without his knowledge, but also pointed out it was unlikely as all units were subject to inspection every three to four months.

Exposed's viewers were then told that *"confidential police documents . . . reveal multiple residents of Wisbeach were never interviewed by detectives"*. Despite referring to multiple residents, only one was identified. He was a Mr Darryl Henson (hereafter "Henson"). Henson was located in New Zealand via a Facebook search. Contact was made and Henson was interviewed by a live video hook up. A photograph of Keli was held up by the interviewer and, without hesitation, Henson identified Keli as a person he *"definitely"* remembered seeing at Wisbeach in 1995 or 1996[140].

An interview was arranged in New Zealand. In this interview Henson described how he was working on his car in the car park underneath the Wisbeach apartment block and *"this lady"* would exit the car park. It would be quite late, sometimes 1.00am. He saw her so many times he thought she lived there. She probably could not see him in the dark. He was confident *"100%"* that he saw her. But there were some formidable problems with what Henson said. In particular, it is hard to believe that in 2018 he would be able to recognise a person who was a

---

[139] *Lane v. R* [2013] NSWCCA 317, at paragraph 252.
[140] *Exposed,* Episode 2, at 0.32.

stranger when he last saw her (in darkness) in 1995/96. It seems even more of a stretch that he was "*100%*" confident of his identification.

There was another major problem with Henson's evidence. Keli herself had stated to Kehoe (in 2001) that when she stayed with "Andrew" she would attend water polo training at Dawn Fraser Pool at Balmain the morning after. Therefore, it would appear she did not leave Wisbeach late at night. Thus, it seems unlikely that Keli was the woman allegedly seen by Henson. For this reason alone, Henson's evidence was unlikely to assist.

Ultimately, Henson's evidence was of such low probative value that it is questionable whether it would even be admissible in the event that it was sought to be tendered by Keli at a trial[141].

The next attempt to discredit the police investigation, in particular the searches, was the revelation that the police did not obtain three months of Keli's phone records (December 1996 to February 1997) which might have disclosed "Andrew's" phone number[142]. It was stated that the phone records had been destroyed. However, *Exposed's* viewers were not told when they were destroyed. For all we know, they had been destroyed <u>before</u> Keli first told police about "Andrew" in 2001, making it impossible for police to have found them.

In any event, the missing phone records begged the question: why had Keli herself not sought her own phone records ? Although there was no obligation upon Keli to prove the existence and whereabouts of "Andrew"/Tegan for the purely legal purpose of defending herself in criminal proceedings, it was puzzling that Keli herself felt no inclination to start searching for her daughter, and start in 1999 when she became aware that Tegan's whereabouts was an issue (if she

---

[141] The *Evidence Act 1995* (NSW) empowers the court to refuse to admit evidence where its probative value is substantially outweighed by the danger the evidence might be unfairly prejudicial. Identification evidence has long been recognised as a type of evidence fraught with the risk of unreliability: see Odgers, S.C., *Uniform Evidence Law*, 13th Edn., Thomson Reuters, 2018, at page 914; *R v. Stafford* [2009] QCA 407. Other extraordinary, and amusing, revelations about Henson's credibility can be found on the Problem Child Podcast. Amongst other things, it transpires that the failure of police to interview Henson was not for want of trying. Police had tried, but been unable, to contact him. It was suspected that this might have been because of his own issues with the law.

[142] *Exposed*, Episode 2, at 0.49ff.

was genuinely unaware of Tegan's whereabouts). Phone records of calls to "Andrew" would have been one of her first ports of call if she was genuinely interested in finding Tegan. When questioned by Kehoe in February 2001, she said she would "*start looking tonight*" for "Andrew's" mobile phone number. And then she told Kehoe it was "*just a matter of going through things*". It did not sound like it would be a difficult search. It might be inferred that her omission to get those records herself in 2001 was an indication that she had no genuine desire to locate "Andrew"/Tegan at all. The further inference might be that Keli knew that trying to locate them would be futile because she knew "Andrew" never existed and Tegan had ceased to exist.

In my research, I have found no evidence of Keli searching for Tegan save for two brief messages advertising in 2004 for "Andrew Norris" on a web site catering for long lost school friends searching for each other. This was reported by a journalist, Kara Lawrence, writing in the Sydney *Daily Telegraph*. Ms Lawrence would later testify that there had been no response to her article about the internet posts.

In fairness to Keli, there was at least one report of her receiving legal advice in 2004 to the effect that engaging a private investigator to find "Andrew" and Tegan would be prohibitively expensive[143]. However, this only goes so far in explaining the virtually complete failure to do anything since 1999. There were other options, short of hiring a private investigator. If Keli had simply told Mr Borovnik about "Andrew" back in 1999, it was conceivable that "Andrew" and Tegan could have been located (if they existed). At that stage, Keli would have had the attention of DOCS to a missing child. That this did not happen had nothing to do with Keli's finances, and much to do with Keli's lies. Likewise, the apparent omission to search for Andrew's phone number, both in 2001 after the interview with Kehoe and later when she told Gaut she would search the boxes at 10 Venus Street, Gladesville were more instances of Keli's lies and lack of cooperation positively hindering the investigation. In short,

---

[143] Langdon, *The Child Who Never Was*, p.79.

had Keli cooperated with DOCS and police, instead of lying and obfuscating, there was some chance "Andrew" and Tegan could have been found (if they existed).

The next matter raised by *Exposed* was that no "comfit" of "Andrew" was ever drawn by the police[144]. A "comfit" is an identikit picture of a person, usually used to identify and locate suspects in criminal investigations. I do not know why a comfit was not drawn. It might be reasonable to suppose that a comfit was never undertaken because it never occurred to police to do so (because Keli herself was the suspect). However, in fairness to *Exposed*, there seems to have been no reason why a comfit ought not to have been drawn. If so, it might qualify as a shortcoming in the investigation. But the notion that a comfit would have achieved anything when the massive searches otherwise undertaken did not reveal anything seems far-fetched. In my opinion, the absence of a comfit was an insignificant blip in what was in truth a meticulous and enormous search effort.

Furthermore, importantly, there seems to have been an overarching misconception on the part of *Exposed* in assuming, and potentially leading viewers to assume, that the police search evidence was the only evidence tendered by the Crown to prove Tegan was deceased. I have not seen, nor would I expect to see, any suggestion by the Crown that the search evidence of itself was capable of proving Tegan was deceased. The search evidence was tendered by the Crown to prove no more than that the police had made a genuine effort to find Tegan alive, and that they had not been successful. It could not, of itself, prove Tegan was deceased. It was a classic example of circumstantial evidence. The Crown asked the jury to consider it together with the other evidence and draw an inference that Tegan must be dead.

Finally, in any event, even if the police investigation was less than optimal, this was not something that caused prejudice to Keli. As the CCA stated:

---

[144] *Exposed*, Episode 2, at 0.57.

". . . it is difficult to see what prejudice was caused to [Keli] by the nature of the investigation. Every lead [Keli] gave to Detective Gaut was followed up. Potential witnesses in her favour, such as Lisa Andreatta, were located and questioned. As it happens, the evidence Ms Andreatta gave did not assist [Keli] at all. But it can hardly be said that a substandard investigation caused prejudice to [Keli]. It was evidence that the investigation yielded that caused prejudice, but it was not in any way unfair prejudice"[145]

In summary, the police investigation was not deficient, and the "incompleteness" of the searches was of no consequence.

Claim 13 – Keli's Lawyers Were Incompetent

To some extent, I have already covered this ground. I apologise in advance if the following is repetitive.

There was veiled, and in my opinion odious, insinuation in *Exposed* that Keli was the victim of negligence by her lawyers in the way they conducted her case. Keli's solicitor, one Ben Archbold, was lampooned for having participated in a reality television show. Chapple SC, and another solicitor, were made to look suspicious for not returning phone calls or agreeing to involve themselves in the documentary. They were made to look like they had things to hide. But not a skerrick of evidence of negligence or other wrongdoing was presented. It was all done by shadowy insinuation. It was done by raising seeds of doubt about the lawyers. If what I have seen on social media is any indication, these seeds have germinated – one internet site has announced quite prominently that Mr Archbold has questions that he should answer. As this book goes to press, and as *Exposed* is circulated to a worldwide audience, the internet continues to be alight with defamatory statements about the defence lawyers.

I have seen nothing to suggest negligence on the part of any of the lawyers who represented Keli. The CCA judgment set out the

---

[145] *Lane v. R* [2013] NSWCCA 317, at paragraph 290.

ways in which the defence counsel, I think skilfully, attempted to spin the facts in Keli's favour. The CCA referred to the defence counsel addressing the jury *"comprehensively and in considerable detail on the evidence"*[146]. For my part, with respect, I thought Mr Chapple SC did exceedingly well to succeed at first instance on the argument about the admissibility of the lies as consciousness of guilt. None of this was consistent with incompetence. If my interpretation of the defence lawyers' conduct of the case is correct, that is to say their strategy was to tacitly accept that Keli had told lies, but fight the case on the basis that she should not be convicted for murder for being a liar, then, in my opinion, they conducted the defence in the right way.

It is trite to say that people may have good reasons for not talking to the media. They may apprehend that their comments will be taken out of context or will not be understood. And so on. If people choose not to talk to the media, their silence should not be used against them. The silence of Keli's lawyers should not have been used to insinuate there was anything sinister or negligent done by them.

---

[146] *Lane v. R* [2013] NSWCCA 317, at paragraph 269.

Chapter 4 - Conclusions

Where is Tegan?

As this book is written, it is 23 years since the last confirmed sighting of baby Tegan. It is 14 years since the inquest which thrust the affair into the national limelight. It is nine years since Keli was convicted of Tegan's murder in one of the most high-profile criminal trials in the history of this country. For 14 years, there has been extensive, and at times saturation, media coverage of the events on television, radio, newspapers and across the internet. By 2010, there had been 283 articles in 27 Australian newspapers and magazines and 400 online articles (plus blogs and Youtube videos)[147]. There have been many articles since. For four months in 2010, during the trial, the case was nightly news. Despite all of this, no "Andrew Morris" or "Andrew Norris", or anybody, has come forward, nor has anybody been able to verify that Tegan is alive.

Searches by police and other authorities which can only be described as exhaustive over many years have failed to locate "Andrew" or Tegan.

The Coroner's public appeals during the inquest in 2005, accompanied as they were by Centacare's assurance of discretion, failed to elicit "Andrew" or Tegan or anything.

The internet posts on the school friends web site, amplified by the *Daily Telegraph* in June 2005, elicited nothing.

---

[147] Evidence of Detective Tamer Kilani at trial.

In 2011, the Channel 7 program, *Sunday Night*, featured a story about the disappearance of Tegan. It aired in prime time. The program offered a reward of $500,000 for information leading to the location of Tegan. Nobody came forward.

In 2015, a Channel 9 program ran a two part story on the disappearance of Tegan. It aired in prime time. Still no "Andrew" or Tegan came forward, nor anybody who knew them, nor anybody able to say they knew a childless couple who suddenly had a child.

The most plausible inference from all of this is that "Andrew Morris/Norris" never existed and Tegan does not now exist.

In 2018, *Exposed* arrived with what was promoted as a novel documentary approach of engaging its audience to try to solve the "mystery". *Exposed* was accompanied by a substantial amount of promotion, both before and after its broadcast in 2018. As well as the standard pre-program advertising, there was the following promotion of *Exposed* and its bid to solve the mystery:

1. Shortly before the first episode, on 25 September, an *Exposed* reporter appeared for an interview on the ABC's News Breakfast program.

2. Immediately after the last episode, on 9 October, two reporters presented a sequel in which they announced they had been *"inundated with hundreds of tips and leads about the identity of Tegan's father and what could have happened to the baby"* since the documentary began. The response to the documentary was described as *"massive"*. It was also announced that, irrespective of the guilt or innocence of Keli, *"we want to get to the bottom of the mystery of where baby Tegan is, dead or alive"*. Then this plea:

   "We need your help to find Tegan's father. Last week we released a forensic sketch of the man [Keli] claims that she gave her baby to, and now <u>we're going to follow up every lead</u> and share our findings with you in our new Facebook group. We're continuing our investigation.

And you can still contact us confidentially via e-mail on exposed@abc.net.au" [emphasis added]

3. There was a "Q & A" on the Facebook page.

4. A reporter was interviewed on a morning show entitled "Studio 10" on a free-to-air television channel.

5. At least one reporter took to Twitter.

6. The documentary featured in a campaign of advertising for ABC's summer programming, available on "iview".

7. There were features on various radio shows.

8. There were stories in the paper media, including various magazines and newspapers, both metropolitan and regional.

9. A "podcast" was undertaken on "Whooshka Fourth Estate" which, I am informed, is a radio station operating from the University of Technology in Sydney.

10. A reporter featured in a podcast on "Mamamia" and was interviewed by a person by the name of Mia Freedman.

11. The documentary was sold and broadcasted internationally.

12. The documentary became available for sale on "itunes".

The excitement continued in the ensuing weeks. An *Exposed* reporter posted this on the Facebook page:

> *"We are following up the thousands of emails, tips and leads we have received. We have actually had some amazing information come through"* [emphasis added]

Despite the *"massive"* response, *"amazing information"* and *"thousands of emails, tips and leads"*, every one of which was going to be followed up, there is still no "Andrew" or Tegan. As this book nears publication, the *Exposed* Facebook group has been archived. I have written to the given e-mail address with an enquiry about what has been followed up or found, but have received no reply.

One is driven to conclude that, if "Andrew" and his mum and "Mel" do exist, they must be huddled together under a proverbial rock.

Never in the annals of crime in Australia, or perhaps anywhere, would there have been so much reaching out, searching for, or imploring of a human being to come forward as there has been for "Andrew Morris/Norris". There has been 14 years of intense media coverage of the events. The case would arguably be the most publicised murder conviction in Australian history. And yet still no sign of "Andrew Morris/Norris".

I am driven to conclude that there was no "Andrew Morris" or "Andrew Norris". There is now, sadly, no Tegan. And the only unanswered questions are (1) how did Keli kill Tegan? and (2) where is Tegan's body? Only Keli knows the answers to these questions and she is unlikely to ever tell.

Causation - why?

Causation is almost always multi-factorial. In this case, there were several layers of motive and cause. It is firstly necessary to seek to understand Keli and the way she lived her life in her teens and early twenties.

A consultant psychiatrist, Dr Michael Diamond, testified before Whealy J on the sentencing of Keli. Unfortunately, he had not been able to examine Keli and his evidence was limited by this circumstance. However, like Whealy J, and with respect, I consider there was value in Dr Diamond's evidence[148]. Dr Diamond considered Keli did not suffer from any recognisable psychiatric condition and there was no relevant impairment of mind and no question that at all times she knew right from wrong. Dr Diamond considered there was a personality disorder, although he could not make any more specific diagnosis. He thought there was a "*repetition compulsion*" in the nature of "*a powerful drive to revisit an unresolved conflict state*". That is, as I understand Dr Diamond's evidence, Keli saw each pregnancy as a

---

[148] I am familiar with Dr Diamond. I have conferred with him. I have examined and cross-examined him. I have always found him a reliable and impressive witness. This gives me added comfort in placing reliance upon his evidence.

means of resolving what had been left conflicted and unresolved from each previous pregnancy. Whealy J referred to it this way:

> "It was designed, [Dr Diamond] explained to bring about a re-enactment of that state, in the hope that a previous unsatisfactory and emotionally distressing experience could be corrected by managing the current one more successfully. Dr Diamond said:
>
> 'The behaviour seems to defy any rational explanation for repeating such a poor choice, yet the compulsion to repeat the behaviour is powerful'"[149]

Dr Diamond also spoke of two unusual features of Keli's personality, namely her ability to shut down emotionally, and to act pragmatically on the "spur of the moment" when a problem could not otherwise be solved. The following passage from Whealy J's sentencing comments, drawn from Dr Diamond's evidence, is illuminating:

> "44. The reports of Dr Diamond . . . allow me to come to a reasonably firm conclusion that [Keli's] decision to bring her daughter's life to an end was made in a situation of some desperation and was contributed to, in part, by the dysfunctional complexities arising from aspects of her disordered personality. Putting it bluntly, she must have found herself in a desperate situation and could see no way out. This aspect of her personality requires recognition . . . in its capacity to have a causal connection with the offence . . .
>
> 45. The Crown argued that [Keli] had family and friends who would have helped her in this difficult situation. That is true. The Crown argued that she was not isolated and that she was a gregarious person with many friends. That is also true. But, for

---

[149] *R v. Lane* [2011] NSWSC 289.

the reasons that Dr Diamond explained, she could not, in real terms, turn to her parents, friends, or her boyfriend. She had, for whatever reason, abandoned the prospect of an adoption in this case, and found it impossible to go back to the hospital to take whatever steps were necessary to place the baby in foster care. A young mother with a less disordered personality, and a more rational ability to function within normal constraints, would have told someone of her problems. She would have approached someone for help and ministration. Such a person would not have attempted to solve the problem on their own. It is clear to me, aided by Dr Diamond's evidence, that Keli could not do this, to a large degree because of the complexities and unusual features of her personality in the particular circumstances in which she found herself. From her perspective, irrational though it was, there was simply no way out.

46. Dr Diamond, in his first report, made a telling point. He was commenting on a situation which had arisen in an interview with Detective Senior Constable Gaut. [Keli] had been interrogated by the police officer about the situation where, at Auburn Hospital, she 'needed to have the pregnancy induced'. Dr Diamond noticed that she became very distressed at this part of the recorded interview. He thought these questions 'were very close to revealing her true distress at the time when she was pregnant with Tegan, had kept the pregnancy secret, had no plan for what she might do with Tegan after the birth'.

47. In his second report, when dealing with an analysis of [Keli's] mental processes during the period of pregnancy and the murder of Tegan, Dr Diamond suggested that [Keli's] emotional outbursts in later years, when she was asked to talk about the disposal of the child, demonstrated very clearly her state of mind that she had no other options and, for whatever reason, she could not present the child to her boyfriend or her parents. Her stated view was that 'she had no other option'. Dr Diamond said that these conversations (and, in particular, the discussion with her then-partner on 9th September 2004) revealed the emotional state of pragmatism and desperation she must have felt on the earlier occasion in 1996.[150]

Whealy J referred to Keli's *"unclassified but real personality disorder"* and concluded that the offence was premeditated but only for a short time:

"It was committed in a sense of desperation arising from a sense of entrapment and isolation, and a perceived inability to communicate with the very people who would have eased her burden and helped her out of the desperate situation in which she found herself. Irrational though these feelings were, I accept that they were likely to have been experienced by the offender"[151]

There was relatively little discussion by Whealy J of Keli's terminations and adoptions. Curiously, he appears to have been reluctant to ascribe a reason for Keli's determination to avoid adoption in the case of Tegan (*"She had, for whatever reason, abandoned the prospect of an adoption [of Tegan]"*). This seems puzzling. The evidence was abundant that Trisha's adoption had been traumatic for Keli.

Keli clearly wanted to avoid both adoption and termination. In particular, plainly I think, the adoption of Trisha was a difficult, if not unbearable, experience for Keli. Not only was there the trauma of visiting Trisha with her adoptive parents, there was also the stress of being pursued by the adoption agency for the signing of Supreme Court affidavits and the like. This was surely something Keli had not anticipated. There was a real possibility the process would bring about exactly what Keli was seeking to avoid – the adoption coming to the notice of family or friends. I have come to the conclusion that Keli

---

[150] *R v. Lane* [2011] NSWSC 289.
[151] *R v. Lane* [2011] NSWSC 289 at paragraph 49.

became very determined to avoid adoption after the experience of Trisha's adoption.

During 1996, Keli procrastinated about the impending birth of Tegan. She compartmentalised the problem, hiding it day in day out, but never coming to grips with what she was going to do with her child when it was born. Adoption and termination had proved traumatic in the past and were to be avoided. But one thing was clear – she was not going to keep a baby. I think it is reasonable to postulate that Keli set the wedding of Duncan's acquaintance on Saturday 14 September as a target by which time the problem had to be sorted. Realistically, she had to be at the wedding, even though she was barely acquainted with the wedding couple[152]. If she missed the wedding, questions would be asked about her whereabouts. And, when at the wedding, she had to be not pregnant and she had to not have a baby. She had to be "not pregnant" because of the risk of going into labour at the wedding, which had happened at the Balmain pub in 1995. She had to "not have a baby" because keeping a baby secret would have been too difficult (even just for the relatively short time involved in attending the wedding and reception). There was also the looming employment at Ravenswood School, due to commence on 9 October.

Time became of the essence. Keli tried hard, but unsuccessfully, to get an induction at Ryde Hospital in the week leading up to Thursday 12th September. Having either procrastinated about adoption for too long or decided against it (probably the latter), Keli found herself in a state of some desperation and shut herself down emotionally (Dr Diamond's evidence). Her ability to act pragmatically, on the spur of the moment, when a problem could not be solved, kicked in. In her own irrational and disordered way, without a great deal of thought about it beforehand (or after), she did what a less disordered person would consider unthinkable – she killed her baby. Later, by the

---

[152] *R v. Lane* [2011] NSWSC 289, at paragraph 42.

time of Archie's birth in 1999, Keli would judge that killing was too unbearably traumatic, and chose adoption. I stress that nothing said in this and the preceding paragraph should be construed as other than my postulation, or opinion, about the events based upon the evidence I have seen.

The postulations in the preceding two paragraphs roughly correspond with the Crown's case theory, although I have come to my views independently. They help to supply the answer to one of the most frequently asked questions about the case – how can the murder of Tegan be reconciled with the adoptions of Trisha and Archie ? In other words, why would Keli murder Tegan when she adopted out Trisha and Archie ? To the extent that it might be doubted that my answer (as above) and/or the Crown's case theory are sufficient to answer the question, I think it suffices to say that the Crown never has to prove guilt beyond all doubt. The standard of proof required of the Crown's case is beyond reasonable doubt. By its nature, crime is an activity where the reasons and thought processes of the alleged perpetrator often remain hidden. The Crown can never be expected to prove every thought or reason behind a crime. In the circumstances of this case, in particular the otherwise strong evidence in favour of guilt for murdering Tegan, the jury would, in my view, have been entitled to leave aside the arguably anomalous pattern of adoption followed by murder followed by adoption. In other words, the jury would have been entitled to find that that pattern, at its highest, did not constitute an hypothesis consistent with innocence.

In any event, the pattern of adoption-murder-adoption was a somewhat treacherous double-edged sword for Keli. Whilst it may have generated an anomalous appearance in the Crown's case, it also exposed the real anomaly in Keli's defence, discussed earlier, that given Keli's need for permanent solution(s) it was, in truth, unlikely that Keli would hand Tegan over to the natural father in circumstances where she wanted to keep the natural fathers of Trisha and Archie out of the picture.

Exposed weighed into the psychological (or potential psychiatric) issues by arranging for Keli to be examined by a forensic psychiatrist who described herself as Professor Anne Buist[153]. Professor Buist claimed to have special expertise in mother/child psychiatric issues and post natal depression. She also claimed to have examined mothers who had murdered children. *Exposed* is to be congratulated on engaging with a suitably qualified specialist. Handled well, this would have been a good opportunity to shed light on the events. But, in my view, it was handled poorly. It only heightened the confusion and threw up more questions than answers.

As to diagnosis, Professor Buist stated that Keli was not mentally ill "*in a diagnostic sense*". Unfortunately, however, this was not explored with Professor Buist. Viewers were left with Professor Buist's opinion about what Keli was <u>not</u>, but were never told what Professor Buist thought Keli <u>was</u>.

The reporter then put a number of "*descriptions*" of Keli to Professor Buist. It was not stated where these descriptions came from. Apparently, Professor Buist was confined to "yes" or "no" comments to signify whether these descriptions fitted Keli. The reporter introduced this segment with the words "*I'm just going to rattle them off*", and that's exactly what she did. This was hardly edifying. In my opinion, the interview was uninformative and belittling of Professor Buist's expertise. Professor Buist would later say that Keli was the hardest case she had ever dealt with, and yet she was being confined to "yes" or "no" comments.

Then followed a sequence in which Professor Buist stated that Keli had got the message from her family that they didn't want to deal with negative emotions – "*they got pushed down, they got squashed*". This statement makes the Lane family sound not unlike many families. The statement may well be correct, but it is seems of little consequence in the constellation of apparently real personality disorder problems that plagued Keli. It does not assist much in understanding why a mother

---

[153] *Exposed* referred to her as Dr Anne Buist. I will refer to her as Professor Buist.

murdered her two day old baby[154]. Ultimately, the interview with Professor Buist did little to shed light on Keli or the murder, and this does not appear to have been through any fault on Professor Buist's part.

My expertise does not allow me to venture further in understanding the psychology of Keli. However, I am equipped to say that she certainly received a fair trial. I cannot detect any error or unfairness to Keli on the part of Whealy J or the jury.

During this project, at times, I have felt sympathy for Keli. I accept the anxiety brought about by pregnancies in her youth. I accept the fear of the parents' possible negative reactions. I understand and empathise with the *"repetition compulsion"* articulated by Dr Diamond. I accept and sympathise with Keli's error prone judgment making. Perhaps more than anything, I accept the torment caused by the media scrum which preyed on her and her family during the inquest in 2005/6 and the trial in 2010.

I also tend to sympathise with Keli's apparent naivety in agreeing to be interviewed for the purposes of *Exposed* and apparently consenting to the broadcast of those interviews. This was unwise, and was presumably done without legal advice[155]. These interviews surrendered information that was harmful to Keli's interests, for example the third different version of the hand-over of Tegan at Auburn Hospital, the uncertainty about the surname of "Andrew" and that "Andrew's" place of residence was in fact only a two minute walk from the pub. They also surrendered admissions about the intensity of the trauma associated with the terminations and first adoption. This was a matter that the Crown had had to prove at the trial. Now it was being proved by Keli's own words – she was confirming the Crown's case.

In my view, whatever slim credibility Keli's story once had was extinguished beyond all hope of rehabilitation by *Exposed*. It might be said that this only demonstrates that *Exposed* was endeavouring to be

---

[154] I mean no criticism of Professor Buist. I perceived she had much to offer on this topic, but was headed off by the editor.

[155] If Keli had legal advice to agree to be interviewed by a television reporter and have the interview/s broadcasted, then I respectfully disagree with such advice.

objective. But I suspect in fact *Exposed* was unaware it was harming Keli's interests in the ways I have set out. Even if I am wrong, and accepting an admirable endeavour to be objective, the documentary was nonetheless substantially inaccurate. Furthermore, at what price should "objective" investigative journalism come ? Should it come at the price of the best interests of its subject (Keli) ? I doubt that it should come at the expense of a person in Keli's predicament surrendering her right to silence, and especially where the person goes on to make damaging admissions. No matter how admirable *Exposed's* endeavours may have been (hypothetically), the documentary has come at a cost to Keli.

Keli was the last person who can be verified as seeing and being with Tegan alive. She was the mother of Tegan. Whether she realised it or not, she found herself in the horns of a dilemma when interviewed by Kehoe in 2001. She had two options – stay silent or say something. If she stayed silent, she probably invited the adverse *Weissensteiner* type of inference discussed earlier. If, on the other hand, she chose to say something, then it needed to be plausible, consistent and preferably corroborated. What Keli in fact delivered was a story that was implausible, littered with inconsistencies and uncorroborated. It is perhaps easy to say this with the benefit of hindsight, but my view is that acquittal was always going to be an uphill battle for Keli.

Exposed was, in my opinion, inaccurate and misleading, largely by dint of what it omitted to tell its viewers. Legitimate questioning of a jury's verdict is one thing. However, questioning of a verdict which has twice been the subject of appellate review, without real reference to the appeal judgments, and by apparently suppressing many of the relevant facts, is quite another. Ultimately, *Exposed* was little more than a recycling of old arguments, long since rejected by the courts, or disavowed by Keli herself, and placing them in 2018 and presumably hoping nobody noticed their antiquity or knew they had been rejected.

The rule of law is the cornerstone of our relatively civil community. It makes it so that disputes are generally solved by pens rather than guns. It marks out Australia as a relatively sophisticated and mature democracy. Maintenance of confidence in the rule of law is crucial. In a democracy, in theory at least, everything is open to question, including the legal system. But care is required. The questioning of the legal system ought not be indiscriminate, as it was in *Exposed*. Otherwise, confidence in the rule of law is unduly eroded. When confidence is lost, other less desirable rules models start to appear attractive. To question a jury conviction sound enough to have been upheld unanimously by the CCA and effectively upheld by the HCA, and to do so inaccurately, was an unwarranted meddling in the rule of law. The introduction of a trial judge who, in effect, disagreed with the verdict of the jury he had instructed, exacerbated the problem. Left uncorrected, all of this was apt to erode confidence in our system of justice and thereby do a disservice to the Australian public.

I do not doubt that the legal system goes pear-shaped from time to time, as all human endeavours are bound to do. But for those wishing to question the system, it is a matter of identifying the right vehicle for inquisition. If the CCA judgment was a split decision or the language of the judgment manifested disquiet about the conviction, then it might be more readily seen that Keli's conviction was open to question. But the judgment was unanimous and the language was unambiguous. Much the same can be said about the HCA's rejection of Keli's application for leave to appeal. There is a remote theoretical possibility that both appeal courts erred, but what the conviction sceptics need to do is confront how these high appeal courts might have got it so wrong. *Exposed* did not even attempt to confront the appeal decisions. It is to be hoped that the noise generated by *Exposed* will not trump the soundness of the outcome delivered by the rule of law.

BIBLIOGRAPHY

Books and Articles

Abrahams, W., *A Guide to Criminal Appeals in New South Wales*, Bar News, Winter 2011, p.73.

Chin, R.J., *Nice Girl*, Simon & Schuster, 2011.

Langdon, A., *The Child Who Never Was*, Park Street Press, 2007.

Odgers, S., *Uniform Evidence Law*, 13th Edn., Thomson Reuters, 2018.

Podcast

"Problem Child", Wicked Podcasts

Authorities and Judgments

Albrighton v. Royal Prince Alfred Hospital [1980] 2 NSWLR 542

Briginshaw v. Briginshaw (1938) 60 CLR 336

Caswell v. Powell Duffryn Associated Collieries Ltd [1940] AC 152

Chamberlain v The Queen [No 2] [1984] HCA 7; (1984) 153 CLR 521

Commonwealth v. Harman 4 Pa St 269

De Gruchy v. R [2002] 211 CLR 85

Demirok v. R (1977) 137 CLR 20

Edwards v. The Queen (1993) 178 CLR 193; [1993] HCA 63

Gilbert v. R [2000] HCA 15; 201 CLR 414

HG v. The Queen [1999] HCA 2; 197 CLR 414

In Re B [1981] 2 NSWLR 372

Lane, Tegan, Inquest Findings of New South Wales State Coroner,
15 February 2006.

Lane v. Queen [2014] HCA Trans 171

Lane v. R [2013] NSWCCA 317

Longman v. The Queen [1989] HCA 60; 168 CLR 79

M v. The Queen (1994) 181 CLR 487

Pointer v. United States [1894] USSC 38; 151 US 396

R v. Birks (1990) 19 NSWLR 677

R v. Demirok [1976] VR 244

R v. Fernando [1999] NSWCCA 66

R v. Hillier [2007] HCA 13; (2007) 233 ALR 634; 81 ALJR 886

R v Lane [No.1] [2010] NSWSC 1528

R v Lane [No.2] [2010] NSWSC 1529

R v Lane [No.3] [2010] NSWSC 1530

R v Lane [No.4] [2010] NSWSC 1531

R v Lane [No.5] [2010] NSWSC 1532

R v Lane [No.6] [2010] NSWSC 1533

R v Lane [No.7] [2010] NSWSC 1534

R v Lane [No.8] [2010] NSWSC 1535

R v Lane [No.9] [2010] NSWSC 1536

R v Lane [No.10] [2010] NSWSC 1537

R v Lane [No.11] [2010] NSWSC 1538

R v Lane [No.12] [2010] NSWSC 1539

R v Lane [No.13] [2010] NSWSC 1540

R v Lane [No.14] [2010] NSWSC 1541

R v Lane [No.15] [2010] NSWSC 1542

R v Lane [No.16] [2010] NSWSC 1543

R v Lane [No.17] [2010] NSWSC 1544

R v Lane [No.18] [2010] NSWSC 1545

R v Lane [No.19] [2010] NSWSC 1546

R v Lane [No.20] [2010] NSWSC 1547

R v Lane [No.21] [2010] NSWSC 1548

R v Lane [No.22] [2010] NSWSC 1549

R v Lane [No.23] [2010] NSWSC 1553

R v Lane [No.24] [2011] NSWSC 72

R v. Lane [2011] NSWSC 289

R v. Lane [2011] NSWCCA 157

R v. Stafford [2009] QCA 407

Richardson v. Queen [1974] HCA 19; 131 CLR 116

Ross v. R [2012] NSWCCA 207

Shepherd v. R (1990) 170 CLR 573

Taylor, Weaver and Donovan 21 Cr App R 20

The King v. Bell [1911] AC 47

Weissensteiner v. R (1993) 178 CLR 217; (1993) HCA 65

POSTSCRIPT

On 3 July 2019, the ABC reported through its internet news outlet that Mr John Borovnik, the DOCS worker who reported the disappearance of Tegan to the police in November 1999, had been the subject of a report by a police officer who ventured his opinion that Mr Borovnik was "irrational" or "obsessed" with the case.

The ABC news item described Mr Borovnik as a key prosecution witness. The gist of it was that the police officer's opinion about Mr Borovnik was reason to question Keli's conviction. The news item appears to have been an attempt to discredit Mr Borovnik.

The ABC report was sketchy. I have not been able to obtain the subject police report. My own information is sketchy, but I am given to understand that Mr Borovnik complained (repeatedly) to the police about the three years of virtual inactivity following his report of Tegan's disappearance. It was Mr Borovnik's repeated complaints, as I understand it, that prompted the police officer to disparage him as "irrational" or "obsessed". The rest of this Postscript proceeds on the assumption that this is correct.

I am compelled to say the following.

Three years elapsed between Mr Borovnik's report to police of a missing two day old baby and the police doing anything about it, save for Detective Kehoe's interview in February 2001. It seems to me that Mr Borovnik had every right to be obsessed about such an appalling state of affairs. Any sensible person would be livid about it. And, incredibly, there is still no satisfactory explanation by the police of which I am aware.

Furthermore, the ABC's description of Mr Borovnik as a key witness was misconceived and misleading. Without wishing to disparage Mr Borovnik, he was not in any relevant sense a "key" prosecution witness. He was an important person in the overall story because he discovered the disappearance of Tegan. But he was not forensically a key witness in the prosecution of Keli. His role was limited and uncontroversial. He was the person who came across the proverbial scene of the crime and reported it to the police. He testified about matters that were not seriously, or at all, in issue between the parties, for example discovering Tegan's birth, suspecting foul play, referring the matter to the police and Keli denying she had a baby in 1996. Keli never seriously contested any of this at the trial. Accordingly, Mr Borovnik's credibility was not an issue. Even if, hypothetically, Mr Borovnik's credibility was reduced to zero, it would not have mattered to the prosecution, or altered the outcome of the trial.

The vice in the depiction of Mr Borovnik as a "key" witness was the same as that in respect of RN Hanlon – both witnesses were promoted to roles that were out of all proportion to the real importance of their evidence at the trial, then ambiguities or other supposed problems with their evidence was used to tarnish the whole of the prosecution.

Even if I am wrong, the opinion held by one prosecution witness (a police officer) about another prosecution witness (a DOCS officer) is of no relevance or assistance. It was for the jury to form its own opinion about Mr Borovnik. It is doubtful, to say the least, that a police officer's opinion about him could be of assistance [156]. Certainly the police officer's opinion was no reason whatsoever to question the conviction.

It is regrettable that Mr Borovnik has been the subject of this news report by the ABC. The circumstances surrounding the police officer's opinion, properly understood, only really serve to highlight the

---

[156] *HG v. The Queen* (1999) HCA 2; 197 CLR 414.

tardiness of the police in not responding to Mr Borovnik's report of Tegan's disappearance. That the police did virtually nothing for three years was appalling. The police should be called to account for this. On the basis of the information at my disposal, Mr Borovnik deserves only praise for pestering the police or being "obsessive" about the case, if that was in fact what happened.